CHRISTIAN DOCTRINE IN GLOBAL PERSPECTIVE

Series Editor: David Smith

Consulting Editor: John Stott

TITLES IN THIS SERIES

The New Global Mission, Samuel Escobar

The Human Condition, Joe M Kapolyo

Evangelical Truth, John Stott

The Bible and Other Faiths, Ida Glaser

Hope for the World, Roland Chia

Salvation Belongs to Our God, Christopher Wright

OTHER BOOKS BY CHRISTOPHER WRIGHT

About the Uniqueness of Jesus

Deuteronomy
(New International Biblical Commentary on the Old Testament)

Knowing Jesus Through the Old Testament

Knowing the Holy Spirit Through the Old Testament

Knowing God the Father Through the Old Testament

Life Through God's Word: Psalm 119

The Message of Ezekiel (The Bible Speaks Today)

The Mission of God: Unlocking the Bible's Grand Narrative

Old Testament Ethics for the People of God

CHRISTIAN
DOCTRINE
IN GLOBAL
PERSPECTIVE

Salvation Belongs to Our God

CELEBRATING THE BIBLE'S CENTRAL STORY

Christopher J. H. Wright

Series Editor: David Smith
Consulting Editor: John Stott

IVP Academic
An imprint of InterVarsity Press
Downers Grove, Illinois

InterVarsity Press
P.O. Box 1400, Downers Grove, IL 60515-1426
World Wide Web: www.ivpress.com
E-mail: email@ivpress.com

InterVarsity Press® is the book-publishing division of InterVarsity Christian Fellowship/USA®, a student movement active on campus at hundreds of universities, colleges and schools of nursing in the United States of America, and a member movement of the International Fellowship of Evangelical Students. For information about local and regional activities, write Public Relations Dept., InterVarsity Christian Fellowship/USA, 6400 Schroeder Rd., P.O. Box 7895, Madison, WI 53707-7895, or visit the IVCF website at <www.intervarsity.org>.

Design: Cindy Kiple
Images: HIP/Art Resource, NY
ISBN 978-0-8308-3306-1

Printed in the United States of America ∞

Library of Congress Cataloging-in-Publication Data

Wright, Christopher J. H., 1947-
    Salvation belongs to our God: celebrating the Bible's central story
/Christopher J. H. Wright.
        p. cm.—(Christian doctrine in global perspective)
    Includes bibliographical references and index.
    ISBN 978-0-8308-3306-1 (pbk.: alk. paper)
    1. Salvation—Biblical teaching. 2. Bible—Criticism,
interpretation, etc. 3. Salvation—Christianity. I. Title.
    BS680.S25W75 2008
    234—dc22

                                                          2008005935

| P | 19 | 18 | 17 | 16 | 15 | 14 | 13 | 12 | 11 | 10 | 9 | 8 | 7 | 6 | 5 | 4 | 3 | 2 | 1 |
| Y | 24 | 23 | 22 | 21 | 20 | 19 | 18 | 17 | 16 | 15 | 14 | 13 | 12 | 11 | 10 | 09 | 08 |

To

Paul

Brother in life and brother in the Lord

Contents

Series Preface 9

Preface 11

1 SALVATION AND HUMAN NEED 15

2 SALVATION AND GOD'S UNIQUE IDENTITY 37

3 SALVATION AND GOD'S COVENANT BLESSING 56

4 SALVATION AND GOD'S COVENANT STORY 87

5 SALVATION AND OUR EXPERIENCE 117

6 SALVATION AND THE SOVEREIGNTY OF GOD 138

7 SALVATION AND THE LAMB OF GOD 178

CONCLUSION 194

Notes 196

Scripture Index 199

Series Preface

THIS BOOK IS ONE OF A SERIES TITLED Christian Doctrine in Global Perspective being published by a partnership between Langham Literature (incorporating the Evangelical Literature Trust) and InterVarsity Press. Langham Literature is a program of the Langham Partnership International.

The vision for the series has arisen from the knowledge that during the twentieth century a dramatic shift in the Christian center of gravity took place. There are now many more Christians in Africa, Asia and Latin America than there are in Europe and North America. Two major issues have resulted, both of which Christian Doctrine in Global Perspective seeks to address.

First, the basic theological texts available to pastors, students and lay readers in the southern hemisphere have for too long been written by Western authors from a Western perspective. What is needed now are more books by non-Western writers that reflect their own cultures. In consequence, this series has an international authorship, and we thank God that he has raised up so many gifted writers from the developing world whose resolve is to be both biblically faithful and contextually relevant.

Second, what is needed is that non-Western authors will write not only for non-Western readers, but for Western readers as well. Indeed, the adjective *global* is intended to express our desire that biblical understanding will flow freely in all directions. Certainly we in the West need to listen to and learn from our sisters and brothers in other parts of the world. And the decay of many Western churches urgently needs an injection of non-Western Christian vitality. We pray that this series will open up channels of communication in fulfillment of the apostle Paul's conviction that it is only *together with all the saints* that we will be able to grasp the dimensions of Christ's love (Eph 3:18).

Never before in the church's long and checkered history has this possibility been so close to realization. We hope and pray that Christian Doctrine in Global Perspective may, in God's good providence, play a part in making it a reality in the twenty-first century.

John R. W. Stott
David W. Smith

Preface

IT IS A PLEASURE AND PRIVILEGE TO CONTRIBUTE a volume to a series which owes its origin to one of John Stott's fertile ideas. The Global Christian Library, or Christian Doctrine in Global Perspective, is a series intended to provide simple and readable surveys of key Christian doctrines, with the contributing authors coming mainly from the Majority World, so that the series as a whole resonates with insights and perspectives from many different global contexts. At the time the series was conceived, John Stott had just invited me to take over the leadership of the Langham Partnership International, and since Langham Literature is the major sponsor of the series, he kindly invited me to contribute this study on salvation. It is offered with thanks to John Stott and appreciation for the value of the other volumes in the series.

Two events contributed to the development of my thinking on the topic. The first was the conference of Anglican leaders and theologians from around the world in July 2002, hosted by Wycliffe College, Oxford, at which I was invited to present a plenary paper on salvation. I chose to adopt a survey of biblical perspectives, starting from the very end of the Bible with the text "Salvation belongs to our God, who sits on the throne, and to the Lamb" (Rev 7:10), and using that as my template. Shortly after, I was invited to deliver The Frumentius Lectures 2005, at the Evangelical Theological College in Addis Ababa, Ethiopia (named after the first missionary bishop of Ethiopia in the fourth century). I developed the same approach further for those lectures. I am grateful to Peter Walker, Steve Bryan and Semeon Mulatu for their invitations and the stimulation they provided for the work which has eventually been consolidated in the following pages. And I thank David Smith and Philip Duce, whose editorial work has helped improve and clarify my initial draft in many ways.

It will be clear that this book strives to treat its topic by gaining a biblical perspective that is as broad as possible. The Bible uses the vocabulary of salvation very widely indeed. I did not want to predetermine what constitutes acceptable theological categories within a structured doctrinal framework. I rather wanted to take that text in Revelation 7:10 and find out what biblical assumptions, content, expectations and implications are nested within its simple phrases. I took the text for many a run and walk, chewing and turning it over again and again in the light of the rest of the Bible story and teaching. The results of meditating deeply on that text in all its biblical resonances were surprisingly comprehensive. I hope the following chapters will enrich readers' grasp of how the Bible itself uses the language of salvation in such multifaceted ways.

Because I spend a lot of time in this book talking about the way the Old Testament speaks of salvation, it is necessary to be very particular about the God who meets us in the pages of the Old Testament. His personal name in Hebrew was YHWH, which in some older Bibles was roughly transliterated as "Jehovah." Scholars nowadays tend to use the name Yahweh as a possible indication of how the original name was pronounced, though nobody can be completely sure. Ever since the Greek translators rendered the Hebrew letters with the title Kyrios, meaning "the Lord," there has been a tradition of translation which in English Bibles results in the use of the LORD, in small caps. I sometimes use Yahweh, or the LORD, where I want to make it very clear that the text is not just talking about God in some general sense but is specifically referring to the named covenant God of Old Testament Israel.

It is also very important to emphasize that when the word *Israel* is used in this book, I am talking about biblical Israel of the Old Testament era, or its theological extension in the New Testament to include all those who through faith in the Messiah Jesus are included in the seed of Abraham. It is impossible to gain a fully biblical perspective on salvation without reference to the great story of God's involvement with the people of Israel in biblical times, his promise to Abraham, the exodus, the covenant at Sinai, the temple and sacrificial system, and of course the messianic promises that lead us to Jesus. But we shall see that the promise of God to and through biblical Israel was a promise that *includes all the nations* in its scope. Indeed, even in the Old Testament itself, *Israel* as the name for the covenant people of God becomes extended, in prophetic anticipation, to include other nations.

Most of all, it needs to be stressed very emphatically that although we do need to speak of Israel, if we are to be faithful to the Bible's own story and teaching, there is *nowhere* in this book where I am referring to the modern Israeli state. That is not part of this discussion at all. In my view great damage is done by those who confuse and conflate the Old Testament Israelites in the canon of the Bible, the contemporary diaspora of ethnic Jews around the world, Judaism as a religion and the modern political state of Israel—as if they were all the same thing, and can carry the same theological affirmations. I do not believe these four entities can or should be simplistically identified in that way. Especially we need to distinguish what we believe the New Testament says about the Jews as the ethnic descendants of Abraham from the claims and actions of the modern state of Israel, and not assume that the former can be simply applied to the latter. So I ask the reader constantly to remember that *Israel* in this book refers exclusively to *biblical* Israel, in the ways that the Bible itself uses the term in both the Old and New Testament (ways which, in my opinion, bear no theological relation to the modern state of that name).

"Salvation belongs to our God," but it is often received through human witnesses. In my own case, though I grew up in a Christian home as the youngest child of missionary parents and heard the gospel from infancy, it was my older brother Paul who once asked me, after Sunday school, whether my name was written in the Lamb's Book of Life. I said I didn't know (and probably did not even know what book he meant). He told me I needed to make sure it was. I asked him how, and he led me to open my heart to receive the Lord Jesus Christ as my Savior. Having known the assurance of my own salvation ever since that moment in my early childhood, I am happy to dedicate this small book on the subject to him, with love and gratitude.

Chris Wright
Easter 2007

1

Salvation and Human Need

THE *GRANDE FINALE* OF ANY GREAT WORK OF MUSIC is usually very moving, as in an opera or the great music and dance sequences of traditional cultures. The closing song or climactic chorus or final dance of a great musical drama usually ends in thunderous applause as the audience feels that the performance has delivered the message of the whole work. As you leave the concert hall or theater or village square, you will hear people humming those last tunes. Sometimes you can't get them out of your head for days. Even in cultures where music and drama take the form of local village art forms, without the need for concert halls and theaters, there is emotional power in the words and music that express the grand themes of life and death, struggle, victory, and hope. Human beings in cultures all over the world turn to music, movement, song and drama whenever they wrestle with the really big things that go beyond merely rational analysis.

The Bible ends with a climactic final chorus. The whole of creation will sing it, and it sums up the message of the whole Bible story. It is the theme song for this book, and we will be looking carefully at the hidden depths of every phrase in it in the chapters that follow. It is not a long song, but it sums up a very long story. It is a song we will not want to get out of our heads, or our hearts, for all eternity. Here it is, from John's vision in Revelation 7:9-10:

> After this I looked and there before me was a great multitude that no one could count, from every nation, tribe, people and language, standing before the throne and in front of the Lamb. They were wearing white robes and were holding palm branches in their hands. And they cried out in a loud voice:
>
> > "Salvation belongs to our God,
> > who sits on the throne,
> > and to the Lamb."

All through this book we will be asking what the Bible means when it uses such phrases. And we begin with the very first word. What would have been in the mind of someone who wrote and sang, "*Salvation* belongs to our God"? What we discover when we track the vocabulary through the Bible is that it has a very broad and comprehensive range of significance—in both Old and New Testaments. The statement "God saves" covers a huge range of realities, situations and experiences. And the reason for this is the immense variety of circumstances in which God's saving engagement with people takes place through the great sweep of biblical history. The fact is, we human beings *need* a lot of saving. And God *does* a lot of saving in the Bible.

Human beings, living as mortal, weak and fallen creatures, have an almost limitless range of needs, in which, or out of which, we constantly call for some form of deliverance or another. We just keep on needing to be rescued, it seems. This is not said in order to demean human worth or dignity. On the contrary, the reason God acts to save us in so many different ways is precisely because God believes we *are worth* saving. God created us in his own image. God loves and cares for us. God is moved to grief and anger by our sin, and moved to compassion by our weakness. And so, God saves us. And the Bible shows so many ways in which God does exactly that.

A glimpse at our modern world underlines the continuing relevance of the biblical message about our need of salvation across a very broad front. We can marvel at the amazing progress of the human race in combating disease, improving living conditions for some, raising standards of justice and equality of opportunity in some cultures, and spreading the benefits of education and literacy. And yet any self-congratulation about such patchy progress is outweighed by the crushing poverty of millions, the scourge of HIV/AIDS along with the resurgence of some older diseases, the appalling brutality and violence that blight the lives of millions in wars great and small, the endless misery of long-term refugees. And to all this we must add the reality of two-thirds of the world's population who have little or no access to any understanding of the salvation that Jesus accomplished through his death and resurrection, and who thus live and die in spiritual ignorance of the gospel. For behind all the manifestations and symptoms of our dire human condition lies the fundamental reality of our sin, our deliberate rebellion against God and all the consequences that it has brought upon us, including what the Bible clearly and repeatedly calls the wrath or anger of God. We *need* to be saved, or else there is simply no hope at any level in the present or the future, in this life or for eternity.

The range of contexts in which the Bible speaks about God's salvation is very wide indeed. We ought to resist the temptation immediately to discount and set aside what we might regard as ordinary or material or earthly instances of the biblical language of salvation and then to isolate only those we might deem theological or transcendent or eternal. That is a form of unbiblical dualism that Christians very quickly fall into.

Now of course we must discern the Bible's own *priorities* within its broad salvation agenda. Some things are certainly more important than others. Certain human needs matter more than others in the end. There are things that we need to be saved from that are more ultimately fatal and destructive than other things. The Bible itself shows that being saved from the wrath of God matters a lot more in the end than being saved from illness or injustice. But the Bible also talks emphatically about *both* as being parts of the saving work of God. We cannot confine the vocabulary of salvation to only one part of what the Bible means by it.

So, yes, we will need to understand those different levels and priorities. But we also need to see the scope of the Bible's salvation agenda as a whole. We need to let the whole biblical witness speak for itself. Biblical salvation involves the whole Bible story and is not just a set of theological doctrines or spiritual experiences. And the Bible's description of God acting in salvation includes the whole of human life in every dimension and is not merely an insurance policy for our souls after death. We need, in other words, to have a *holistic* understanding of salvation. And that too will be a concern of this book all the way through.

SALVATION IN GENERAL

In the Old Testament. In the Old Testament, the verb *yāša'* (to save) and its derivative nouns (especially *yĕšûa'*, salvation), along with the verb *hiṣṣîl* (to deliver), are used in all sorts of contexts. Here are some of them, with examples. In each Scripture quotation I have put in italics the relevant verbs or nouns of salvation, so that we can quickly see the point of each reference.

Deliverance from oppressors or enemies. This is probably the commonest use of all since the history of Israel is littered with such situations and matching acts of God's deliverance. The exodus was the greatest and the prototype of all the others.

> The LORD said, "I have indeed seen the misery of my people in Egypt. I have heard them crying out because of their slave drivers, and I am concerned about their suffering. So I have come down to *rescue* them from the hand of the Egyptians and to bring them up out of that land into a good and spacious land." (Ex 3:7-8)

> Whenever Israel went out to fight, the hand of the LORD was against them to defeat them, just as he had sworn to them. They were in great distress.

Then the LORD raised up judges, who *saved* them out of the hands of these raiders. . . . Whenever the LORD raised up a judge for them, he was with the judge and *saved* them out of the hands of their enemies as long as the judge lived; for the LORD had compassion on them as they groaned under those who oppressed and afflicted them. (Judg 2:15-16, 18)

Victory in battle. Typically, when Israel prayed for God's help in battle, or prayed for the king in that situation, they appealed to God's power to save.

Now I know that the LORD *saves* his anointed;
> he answers him from his holy heaven
> with the *saving* power of his right hand.
Some trust in chariots and some in horses,
> but we trust in the name of the LORD our God.
They are brought to their knees and fall,
> but we rise up and stand firm.
O LORD, *save* the king!
> Answer us when we call! (Ps 20:6-9; see also Ps 33:16-19)

The healing of sickness. Isaiah 38 records the story of Hezekiah's illness that had brought him to the point of death. In response to his prayers and tears, God restores his health (and promises to deliver his city into the bargain, Is 38:6). Hezekiah's song of thanksgiving makes much of the importance of being kept alive in order to praise God among the living. For Hezekiah, to be spared physical death was God's salvation at that point in his life.

The LORD will *save* me,
> and we will sing with stringed instruments
all the days of our lives
> in the temple of the LORD. (Is 38:20)

Rescue from personal enemies, persecutors or detractors. Many of the psalms were born in the stress of personal attack. This may have been

slander, unjust accusation in court, or outright physical threats and per-
secution. In such circumstances, David and other psalmists did not re-
sort to vengeance, taking the law into their own hands, but entrusted
themselves to God. God would save them. That is, they looked to God
to vindicate and defend them from such assaults, whatever they were.
The language of salvation is commonly used to express this appeal. God
himself used it in responding to Jeremiah when he cried out to God
against those who made his life such a misery.

> O LORD my God, I take refuge in you;
>> *save and deliver* me from all who pursue me,
> or they will tear me like a lion
>> and rip me to pieces with no one to rescue me. . . .
> My shield is God Most High,
>> who *saves* the upright in heart. (Ps 7:1-2, 10)

> "I will make you [Jeremiah] a wall to this people,
>> a fortified wall of bronze;
> they will fight against you
>> but will not overcome you,
> for I am with you
>> *to rescue and save* you," declares the LORD.
> "I will *save* you from the hands of the wicked
>> and *redeem* you from the grasp of the cruel." (Jer 15:20-21)

Vindication in court. The experience of being wrongly accused is not
only painful but can be life-threatening, depending on the seriousness of
the false accusation. Or, if one appeals to the judges in order to receive
justice in a situation of oppression or exploitation, only to be denied that
justice and further marginalized, then that too is deeply destructive—individually and socially. In such situations, Israelites directed their appeal
to God for salvation—to be saved from injustice in the most literal way.

One way in which God would exercise his saving power in society
would be by ensuring that the appointed king—the head of the judicial

system—would himself act justly. Accordingly, Psalm 72 prays that God would endow the king with his own justice and righteousness. Only then would the human king act as the savior of the poor and needy. So, in these verses, the king is seen as the agent of God's salvation, in the social and economic realm. God is the source of the salvation (understood as being rescued from injustice), even though a human being (the king, or government) is the agent of it.

> He will defend the afflicted among the people
> > and *save* the children of the needy;
> > he will crush the oppressor. . . .
> He will take pity on the weak and the needy
> > and *save* the needy from death. (Ps 72:4, 13)

In other cases, God is simply said to act directly as judge in order to save the needy:

> From heaven you pronounced judgment,
> > and the land feared and was quiet—
> when you, O God, rose up to judge,
> > to *save* all the afflicted of the land. (Ps 76:8-9)

So then, to speak of God saving a person or people in the Old Testament can refer to many different ways in which he brings them out of dangerous or negative circumstances into freedom or security.

In the New Testament. In the New Testament, the Greek verb *sōzō* (to save) and its associated noun *sōtēria* (salvation) can be used in a similarly broad sense. And this can be the case even when it is used with God as subject. That is, God can save people in the same kind of general way that we saw above in Old Testament texts. It is a false distinction to say that in the Old Testament salvation was national or physical, whereas in the New Testament it becomes only spiritual and individual. Again, that kind of dualism is foreign to the Bible. Both testaments speak of salvation in these broad and general terms. Here again are some examples.

Rescue from drowning. Twice Jesus responded to people in danger of drowning who cried out to him to save them. In the second case, involving Peter in particular, the story has undoubtedly been told with some metaphorical and spiritual parallels in mind—as many sermons have discerned. But, just as undoubtedly, it was from literal drowning in physical water that Peter wanted physical salvation! He was not asking to be saved so that he could go to heaven when he died, but to be saved from dying right there and then.

> Without warning, a furious storm came up on the lake, so that the waves swept over the boat. But Jesus was sleeping. The disciples went and woke him, saying, "Lord, *save* us! We're going to drown!" (Mt 8:24-25)

> But when he [Peter] saw the wind, he was afraid and, beginning to sink, cried out, "Lord, *save* me!" (Mt 14:30)

Getting better from terminal illness. When the disciples thought that Lazarus was only asleep, not actually dead, they hoped he would thereby recover from illness—which they describe as "being saved." This is very similar to what we found in the psalms and the prayer of Hezekiah.

> He [Jesus] went on to tell them, "Our friend Lazarus has fallen asleep; but I am going there to wake him up." His disciples replied, "Lord, if he sleeps, he will *get better* [lit. 'he will be saved']." (Jn 11:11-12)

Being healed of disease or disability. The Gospels use *sōzō* with probably deliberate ambiguity in the many accounts of Jesus' healing miracles. Sometimes the emphasis is clearly on physical healing (just as in the Old Testament):

> She said to herself, "If I only touch his cloak, I will be *healed.*" Jesus turned and saw her. "Take heart, daughter," he said, "your faith has *healed* you." And the woman was *healed* from that moment. (Mt 9:21-22; all three times, *healed* is actually *saved* in Greek)

Sometimes the emphasis is more on the spiritual dimension behind the illness (Mk 2:1-12). And sometimes it is likely that both physical and spiritual aspects are involved, with the latter dominant (Lk 7:36-50). Above all, the Sabbath day is the time *par excellence* to "save life," which in context means, to heal the sick (Mk 3:1-5).

Being rescued from death. The Gospels record possibly the most ironic use of salvation language in the Bible. At the very moment when Jesus was giving his life for the salvation of the world, people all around him mocked him, by taunting him to save himself—i.e., to save himself from the suffering and inevitable death of the cross.

> The people stood watching, and the rulers even sneered at him. They said, "He saved others; let him *save* himself if he is the Christ of God, the Chosen One."
>
> The soldiers also came up and mocked him. They offered him wine vinegar and said, "If you are the king of the Jews, *save* yourself."
>
> There was a written notice above him, which read: THIS IS THE KING OF THE JEWS.
>
> One of the criminals who hung there hurled insults at him: "Aren't you the Christ? *Save* yourself and us!" (Lk 23:35-39)

The profound irony is especially apparent in the demand of one of the rebels crucified beside him: "Save yourself and us!" That was exactly the point. Jesus could not do both. He could not save himself *and* us. He could have saved *himself*—by the instant summoning of legions of angels to deliver him from his unjust execution. But in that case he could not save us, or anyone else, from the just deserts of our own rebellion. Or he could go ahead and accomplish salvation for *us*. But in that case he could not save himself. For, as he had repeatedly said, the very purpose of his coming was to give his life for the salvation of others. So, against all the taunting, Jesus steadfastly persisted in not saving himself, but rather surrendered his life so that he could save us.

Being rescued from physical and spiritual dangers. Paul, with all his rich theological vocabulary of salvation, could use similar vocabulary quite naturally, and with God as subject, to describe his own recent experiences of rescue from combined physical and spiritual danger, enmity and attack—very much like the language of the psalms.

> We do not want you to be uninformed, brothers, about the hardships we suffered in the province of Asia. We were under great pressure, far beyond our ability to endure, so that we despaired even of life. Indeed, in our hearts we felt the sentence of death. But this happened that we might not rely on ourselves but on God, who raises the dead. He *has delivered* us from such a deadly peril, and he *will deliver* us. On him we have set our hope that he *will continue to deliver* us. (2 Cor 1:8-10; "deliver" is the verb *rhyomai*)

SALVATION FROM SIN

So in both Testaments, then, God saves people in a wide variety of physical, material and temporal ways from all kinds of need, danger and threat. But of course, and also in both Testaments, God's saving action goes much further. It is not that such things are not real problems and dangers in themselves. They certainly are, and God himself takes seriously our need to be saved from them. Whole swaths of the biblical narrative are given to stories of God acting to save people from "ordinary" earthly suffering, need and danger of all kinds. These are real things, and God really saved people from them. But the Bible recognizes that all those proximate evils from which God saves his people are manifestations of the far deeper disorder in human life. There is something that lies behind and beneath all these symptoms of our human predicament.

Think of the things listed above:

- enemies
- lies
- disease
- oppression
- false accusation

- violence

- death

These are all things from which people in the Bible prayed to be saved—and rightly so. And God heard their prayers and frequently acted to deliver them from exactly these things. But all of them, in their deepest roots, are also the results of rebellion and sin in the human heart. That is where the deepest source of the problem lies—as the earliest stories in the Bible had made very clear. Human rebellion and disobedience against God have injected their dismal effects into every dimension of the human *person,* into every dimension of human *society* and into the ongoing sad story of human *history,* escalating with every generation.

There is, therefore, an ultimate need for God to deal with *sin*—sin in the world and sin in his own people. *The biblical God who saves is the God who deals with sin.* We might call this the truly *radical* dimension of the Bible's teaching on salvation. The salvation that this God offers is salvation that first diagnoses where the real *roots* of our problems lie, and then goes right to those roots and deals with them—not merely with their unwelcome fruit. Other claimed salvations of other posturing gods are tinkering cosmetics that leave the real problem untouched. So we need to look at what both testaments have to say about salvation from sin. It is very good news indeed.

Salvation from sin in the Old Testament. Again it is important to insist that this—salvation from sin—is not just a New Testament perspective. Old Testament Israelites knew about the radical depths of sin, and they also knew that only Yahweh's grace could cleanse the parts that other remedies, including their own sacrificial system, could not reach.

The psalmists are unsurpassed in their profound awareness of personal sin and the need for forgiveness and cleansing:

Blessed is he
　　whose transgressions are forgiven,
　　whose sins are covered.

Blessed is the man
   whose sin the LORD does not count against him
   and in whose spirit is no deceit. (Ps 32:1-2)

Have mercy on me, O God,
   according to your unfailing love;
according to your great compassion
   blot out my transgressions.
Wash away all my iniquity
   and cleanse me from my sin.
For I know my transgressions,
   and my sin is always before me. (Ps 51:1-3)

Equally they rejoiced in God's ability to remove sin totally and re-member it no more:

He does not treat us as our sins deserve
   or repay us according to our iniquities.
For as high as the heavens are above the earth,
   so great is his love for those who fear him;
as far as the east is from the west,
   so far has he removed our transgressions from us. (Ps 103:10-12)

Such a feat of permanent forgiveness inspired Micah to a more mari-time metaphor:

You will tread our sins underfoot
and hurl all our iniquities into the depths of the sea. (Mic 7:19)

Isaiah realized that nothing but his sovereign grace enabled God, in the face of Israel's entrenched and incorrigible rebellion, to simply affirm that God would blot out the sins that had so offended him.

I, even I, am he who blots out
   your transgressions, for my own sake,
   and remembers your sins no more. (Is 43:25)

But such grace was not without cost, since it would be the mission of the LORD's servant to *bear* that sin and iniquity, indeed to make his own life a guilt offering in doing so (Is 53:10-12).

Ezekiel looked forward to the day when God would cleanse Israel from sin, giving the people of Israel a new heart and a new spirit (Ezek 36:24-28)—a transformation that would be nothing short of resurrection (Ezek 37).

Thus even death itself, with its shroud of tears—death that had been God's decreed verdict on sin in the Garden of Eden—even death would eventually be destroyed. Isaiah's promise finds its ultimate fulfillment in the words of God himself in Revelation 21:4.

> On this mountain he will destroy
>   the shroud that enfolds all peoples,
> the sheet that covers all nations;
>   he will swallow up death forever.
> The Sovereign LORD will wipe away the tears
>   from all faces;
> he will remove the disgrace of his people
>   from all the earth.
>   The LORD has spoken. (Is 25:7-8)

The post-exilic period brought an even greater longing for a final solution to the problem of sin, and recognition that only God could provide it. But that day would come. "On that day a fountain will be opened to the house of David and the inhabitants of Jerusalem, to cleanse them from sin and impurity" (Zech 13:1).

That would be the day when the one anointed by God would "finish transgression, . . . put an end to sin, . . . atone for wickedness, and . . . bring in everlasting righteousness" (Dan 9:24).

So the Old Testament knew all about the inner spiritual realities of sin and, equally profoundly, knew about the solution to sin—nothing less than the saving forgiveness of Yahweh, the God of Israel. No wonder

Micah asked the rhetorical question, echoing the meaning of his own name (*Micah,* in Hebrew, means "who is like Yahweh?"):

> Who is a God like you,
>   who pardons sin? (Mic 7:18)

Who indeed?

Salvation from sin in the New Testament. The passages we have just surveyed were among the great hopes and expectations, accumulating through Old Testament Israel's history and Scriptures, with which the Gospel writers surrounded the coming of Jesus. They longed for God to come and do something about the problem of sin. And in Jesus, they realized, God was bringing in the promised new era of salvation, for his Old Testament people Israel and for the world. It would be an era of ultimate salvation only and precisely because through Jesus God would deal finally and fully with sin. There could be no final salvation without a final solution to sin. And only God could accomplish that.

In preparation. John the Baptist, in preparation for the coming and ministry of Jesus, preached a message of repentance and forgiveness of sin (Mt 3:6), while pointing to Jesus as the one who "takes away the sin of the world" (Jn 1:29). Matthew records the angel's explanation of the name *Jesus (Jehoshua),* "because he will save his people from their sins" (Mt 1:21).

Luke, however, goes the furthest in festooning the language of salvation around the arrival of Jesus, in what Howard Marshall calls his "overture to the story of salvation." The birth narratives of Luke's Gospel, Marshall says, "function like an overture, setting out the main themes of the following drama, but doing so with their own distinctive music. One of the most characteristic tones here is that of salvation."[1] Luke uses salvation terms seven times in his first three chapters:

- in Mary's song (Lk 1:47)

- in Zechariah's song (Lk 1:69, 71, 77)

- in the angel's announcement to the shepherds (Lk 2:11)

- in Simeon's song (Lk 2:30)

- in Luke's own quotation from Isaiah 40 (Lk 3:6)

This newborn Jesus is, above all else, the salvation of God arrived on earth.

Matthew. Matthew's account of Jesus' encounter with the rich young man equates salvation with inheriting eternal life and entering the kingdom of God (Mt 19:16, 23, 25).

> Now a man came up to Jesus and asked, "Teacher, what good thing must I do to get *eternal life?*" . . . Then Jesus said to his disciples, "I tell you the truth, it is hard for a rich man to enter *the kingdom of heaven.* . . . When the disciples heard this, they were greatly astonished and asked, "Who then can *be saved?*" (Mt 19:16, 23, 25, my italics)

Salvation, for Matthew, thus embraces the totality of enjoying life under the reign of God along with the rest of his restored people who have been saved.

Luke. Luke records Jesus announcing that salvation had come that very day to Zacchaeus's household, because of his response to the challenging presence of Jesus in his home.

> Zacchaeus stood up and said to the Lord, "Look, Lord! Here and now I give half of my possessions to the poor, and if I have cheated anybody out of anything, I will pay back four times the amount."
>
> Jesus said to him, "Today *salvation* has come to this house, because this man, too, is a son of Abraham. For the Son of Man came to seek and to *save* what was lost." (Lk 19:8-10, my italics)

Zacchaeus demonstrated his repentance through a combination of returning to the standards of the law (restoring fourfold what he had stolen—as prescribed in Ex 22:1) and going way beyond the law into the realms of kingdom generosity (giving half his goods to the poor)—an action by which he moved spontaneously in the direction that the rich young man had refused to go.

Significantly, Jesus links his declaration of salvation to Abraham. Zacchaeus is now a genuine child of the Abrahamic covenant because he has entered into the realm of salvation through his response to Jesus. Without such a response to Jesus, Zacchaeus would have remained among the unsaved and the lost—in spite of being an ethnic Israelite, physically descended from Abraham. Only by welcoming Jesus the Messiah did he belong to the true Abrahamic Israel, those whom Jesus had come to seek and to save.

We might also note, in relation to the claims that are made in the teaching of prosperity theology (to which we will return later), that for Zacchaeus being saved did not increase his wealth but cut his riches very significantly. While he was wallowing in his increasing prosperity, Zacchaeus was, in Jesus' terms, *lost*—a disobedient sinner. Through his repentance he was, in Jesus' terms, *saved*—and restored to an obedient covenant lifestyle of honesty and generosity. Salvation for Zacchaeus reduced his wealth but increased his godliness. Prosperity teaching often seems to do the reverse.

John. John widens the scope from Israelites to include the whole world in his classic summary of the gospel:

> For God so loved the world that he gave his one and only Son, that whoever believes in him shall not perish but have eternal life. For God did not send his Son into the world to condemn the world, but to save the world through him. (Jn 3:16-17)

With some irony, John also puts this same message on the lips of the hated Samaritans. Through the testimony of a marginalized woman who had learned from Jesus that "salvation is from the Jews" (Jn 4:22), the people of her town come to testify further that Jesus is in fact nothing less than "the Savior of the world" (Jn 4:42).

John also makes it very clear that salvation means being saved *from* the wrath and judgment of God (as is clear also from the preaching of John the Baptist). *Salvation* is not merely a code word for a happy life.

There is a terrifying reality *from which* we need to be saved. The consequences of our sin and unbelief are that we stand already under the just condemnation of God and will ultimately suffer the irrevocable verdict in the final judgment. The only alternative to being saved and having eternal life is to perish deservedly under God's condemnation. We must therefore accept God's salvation now, through Jesus, in order to be saved from the wrath to come. Salvation and judgment are the clear binary opposites in John's theology (as indeed in the whole New Testament). They form the nonnegotiable background to the gospel he wants his readers to hear and believe. God's judgment is the inescapably bad news without which the good news has no real meaning, or even reason for existence. There is only one alternative to being saved, and Jesus spells it out—final condemnation:

> As for the person who hears my words but does not keep them, I do not judge him. For I did not come to judge the world, but to save it. There is a judge for the one who rejects me and does not accept my words; that very word which I spoke will condemn him at the last day. (Jn 12:47-48)

Paul. For Paul the climax of God's covenant with Old Testament Israel was that, through the sin-bearing death of the Messiah Jesus, salvation was now available to those among the Jews who would believe in him and, through Jesus also, salvation was now available also to people from any and every nation. This was exactly what had been promised in the Old Testament Scriptures—specifically to Abraham. Salvation would *come from* Israel (i.e., through the story of God's dealings with Israel in the Old Testament), but salvation could never be *limited to* Israel (as an ethnic Jewish community). The promise God made to Old Testament Israel had the rest of the world in view from the very start. But Israelites themselves, as one of the nations of the earth, also stood in need of God's salvation and could find it only through their Messiah, Jesus of Nazareth.

Paul's longing and prayer, therefore, which was entirely scriptural in its roots, shape and content, was that God would save his ancient people

Israel: "Brothers, my heart's desire and prayer to God for the Israelites is that they may be saved" (Rom 10:1).

How many psalmists and prophets in Old Testament days had prayed that before Paul? And in that longing Paul was also at one with the prayers of his own contemporary first-century Jewish people everywhere. Where Paul differed was in seeing clearly that the answer to their prayer lay in the crucified Messiah, Jesus from Nazareth. Only through the Messiah Jesus would God save Israel—then, now or ever. Indeed, in Jesus God had *already* saved Israel, and demonstrated it in his resurrection. For in the resurrection of the Messiah, Paul realized, God had *already* fulfilled his promise of restoration to Old Testament Israel. "We tell you the good news: What God promised our fathers he has fulfilled for us, their children, by raising up Jesus" (Acts 13:32-33).

We cannot and should not talk about the restoration of Israel without seeing what the New Testament says about it in relation to the resurrection of Jesus Christ. For that is emphatically how Paul understood the matter. The resurrection of the Messiah is the way God fulfilled his promises to Old Testament Israel, says Paul.

Where Paul further differed from his Jewish contemporaries who had not accepted Jesus as Messiah was in seeing that, in the glorious mystery of God's saving purposes for the world, it was precisely the current hardening of some in *Israel* that was leading to the ingathering of the *nations*. This was the very thing promised of old in the Scriptures, and it was now taking place through the Gentile mission, his own mission as the apostle to the Gentiles: "Because of their [Israel's] transgression, *salvation* has come to the Gentiles" (Rom 11:11, my italics).

The terrible irony, which grieved Paul to the core in its negative force, just as it excited him to the heavens in its positive truth, was that in rejecting the salvation that should have been theirs in Christ (as the fulfillment of all the Old Testament covenant promises), unbelieving Jews were opening the door for precisely the same salvation going to the nations. What Paul further believed, however, was that the ingathering of the Gentiles would ultimately lead to an ingrafting of Jews, such that "all Israel" would be saved in Christ (Rom 11:26).

Paul's letters were mostly written to communities of such Gentile believers—i.e., representatives of the non-Jewish nations who were now being gathered in to the people of God, in fulfillment of God's promise to Abraham. So he could tell the Gentile Christians of Ephesus that they were saved by the grace of God—just as the Old Testament described the salvation of Israel. "For it is by grace you have been saved, through faith—and this not from yourselves, it is the gift of God—not by works, so that no one can boast" (Eph 2:8-9).

But then Paul goes on to explain in detail what an incredible transformation this salvation has produced in the circumstances of these non-Jewish converts. At one level, the Gentiles were no different from the Jews, for (as Paul also says in Rom 3:23) "all have sinned and fall short of the glory of God." So, just like Paul himself and his fellow Jews, these foreign peoples had lived a life of death—spiritually dead, influenced by Satan from without and driven by sinful desires from within (Eph 2:1-3). That much was common to all humanity. And the only answer to that condition, for Jew and Gentile alike, was to be made alive through the love and mercy of God, and through the death, resurrection and ascension of Jesus (Eph 2:4-10).

But for the Gentiles it was even worse in terms of their previous exclusion from what God had been doing in Old Testament Israel. Listen to Paul's assessment of their "B.C." state (i.e., before they came to faith in Jesus):

> Therefore, remember that formerly you who are Gentiles by birth . . . remember that at that time you were separate from Christ, excluded from citizenship in Israel and foreigners to the covenants of the promise, without hope and without God in the world. (Eph 2:11-12)

This is a picture of desperate alienation and exclusion. Non-Jewish pagan Gentiles were

- separated from Israel's Messiah

- separated from Israel's community
- separated from Israel's covenant promises
- separated from Israel's hope
- separated from Israel's God

> *But now* in [the Messiah] Christ Jesus you who once were far away have been brought near through the blood of Christ. (Eph 2:13)

In other words, through the cross of the Messiah and the preaching of the gospel,

- the separated have been connected
- the alienated have been reconciled
- the far away have been brought near
- the outsiders have been brought in

One new humanity has been created and presented to God through Christ (Eph 2:14-18). As a result, those who were formerly languishing in bleak unbelonging have now become

- fellow citizens of God's own country
- members of God's own family
- the place of God's own dwelling

Listen to it in Paul's own words:

> Consequently, you [Gentiles] are no longer foreigners and aliens, but fellow citizens with God's people and members of God's household, built on the foundation of the apostles and prophets, with [the Messiah] Christ Jesus himself as the chief cornerstone. In him the whole building is joined together and rises to become a holy temple in the Lord. And in him you too are being built together to become a dwelling in which God lives by his Spirit. (Eph 2:19-22)

All these images and comparisons are strongly scriptural and covenantal categories. This is Old Testament language now being applied to the whole new people of God in Christ. This is the glorious texture of what Paul means by salvation. Salvation is the miraculous extension to people from all nations of the great covenant truths of Old Testament Israel, now made available to all those who trust in the Lord Jesus Christ— Jews and Gentiles alike, equally and together.

No wonder Paul stands shoulder to shoulder with the Gospel writers in seeing salvation as the central and climactic point of the incarnation. Why was Jesus born? Why did God enter the world in human flesh? For this one reason, says Paul, when he quoted the memorable "trustworthy saying"—"Christ Jesus came into the world *to save sinners*" (1 Tim 1:15).

So, as we review the sweep of this whole chapter, we can see the breadth of the biblical language of salvation. It is holistic. That is, the salvation that the Bible talks about takes in the whole of life, the whole of human need. It encompasses individuals and nations. It addresses the depths of the human person and the breadth of human society. It spans the realms of the physical and the spiritual; the past, the present and the future; the historical and the eternal; this life and the world to come.

We ought to preserve and affirm this biblical totality of God's saving action. We should not split it up, or assign terms like *theological* or *spiritual,* to only one of its dimensions. Ultimately the biblical God has saved, does save and will save his people and his world at every level of our humanity and createdness. And, ultimately, all of God's saving work is founded upon the person and work of Christ.

For salvation is all of grace, and all God's grace is grace in Christ.

QUESTIONS FOR REFLECTION OR DISCUSSION

1. In what ways has this chapter broadened your understanding of the scope of salvation, as the Bible describes it? At what particular points has this challenged your previous understanding?

2. "Salvation for Zaccheus reduced his wealth but increased his godliness. Prosperity teaching often seems to do the reverse." How do you

respond to this point in relation to the way salvation is preached in your own context? Reflect further on the words of Jesus to Zacchaeus, "Salvation has come to this house" in relation to what Zacchaeus said and did.

3. In your local context, what will it mean to bring the good news of salvation in all its biblical dimensions?

2

Salvation and God's Unique Identity

IN CHAPTER ONE WE HAVE SEEN THAT IT IS IMPORTANT, when we talk about *salvation*, to be sure that we are using the word in the way that the Bible does. The same thing is true when we talk about God. We need to be sure what *God* we are talking about. Throughout this book we are engaged in a biblical survey, and so it is important to begin by stressing that whenever we use the word *God* we are talking about the God revealed in the Bible. This may seem rather obvious, but unfortunately there is a great deal of confusion when people use the word *God*—or whatever equivalents exist in other languages. Merely using the right word does not mean we have the right understanding. Some people who say they "believe in God" would be surprised to find out what the Bible actually teaches about the living God. Others who say they "do not believe in God" might also be surprised to discover that the god they do not believe in is equally nonexistent in the Bible too.

This is one of the reasons why I chose Revelation 7:10 as our control text for our study. This text makes it very clear that those whom John witnesses celebrating salvation know exactly *who* has saved them. "Salvation belongs to *our God*"—by which they mean the God whom we know through the whole journey of the Bible story, from creation to new creation. They are not just chanting some religious mantra—"salvation is religion-thing." They are defining very specifically the God to whom salvation belongs.

So in this chapter we explore two aspects of this statement. On the one hand, "salvation *belongs to . . . God."* That is, salvation is God's property, not ours. And on the other hand, "salvation belongs to *our God."* That is, salvation is part of God's identity—he is the saving God (as no other god is).

SALVATION AS THE PROPERTY OF GOD

Our key text makes the very important statement that "salvation *belongs to . . . God."* The form of the words in the doxology of Revelation 7:10 is very Hebraic. That is to say, it is exactly how an Old Testament Israelite would have expressed himself. Literally, the text says, "salvation, to our God." This was the way Hebrew expressed a possessive relationship (as also in French, for example: *ce livre est à moi;* literarily, "this book is to me," i.e., "this book is mine"). It is the same structure as the opening words of Psalm 24, "To Yahweh, the earth and all its fullness"—i.e., the earth belongs to Yahweh; "The earth is the LORD's"; it is his property. Or Deuteronomy 10:14, "To the LORD your God belong the heavens, even the highest heavens, the earth and everything in it." The earth, indeed the whole universe, is "to the LORD"—i.e., it belongs to him. That is what the great multitude of the redeemed will be singing about salvation. Salvation, like everything in the universe, belongs to God. Salvation is God's property. Nobody else owns it.

This is the first point we need to understand then. We tend to think of salvation as something centering on ourselves: We are the ones who need to "get saved"; we want to know how to find salvation; we tell others about how we found salvation, and how they can too. But from beginning to end, we should remember, salvation is something that belongs to God, not to us. Salvation is God's property.

Salvation has God at the center. We could call this the *theocentric* (or

God-centered) dimension of biblical salvation. When the Bible talks about salvation, God is the key, the center, the prime actor. Because salvation, according to the Bible, is the property of God, then this means that salvation can never be a matter of *human* initiation or human achievement. Salvation is not something that we human beings can accomplish or earn by any means, *even including religion*. Salvation is in God's hands. It is not something that any human religion can offer as a reward for doing this or that ritual, or following this or that practice. Salvation belongs to God, not to any religion.

Salvation, as biblically understood, is not at human disposal or a matter of human achievement.

• We do not own or control salvation.

• We cannot dispense salvation to others.

• We certainly cannot sell salvation or offer it on our own terms (though many religions do so—including some perverted forms of Christianity down through the ages).

• We are not the ones who decide who gets to have salvation, or not.

• We cannot threaten or take away salvation from those to whom God has granted it. It is God's decision and gift, not ours.

Salvation belongs to God. According to the Bible, as we shall see throughout this book, salvation is

• initiated by God's grace

• achieved by God's power

• offered on God's terms

• accomplished by God's Son

• secured by God's promises

• guaranteed by God's sovereignty

God is the *subject* of the act of saving us. God is not the *object* of our attempts to gain salvation for ourselves. That is to say, God freely offers to save us; we do not manipulate him to try to extract salvation from him. Salvation is the result of no action of ours other than that of asking and accepting it from God.

This essential biblical perspective on salvation contrasts with religions (including deficient forms of popular Christianity) in which salvation (defined in all kinds of different ways, of course) is something that humans strive toward. Religions prescribe many routes by which we are told we can find or achieve our own salvation. One very popular metaphor that is used again and again is that all the different religions are like different paths up a mountain. Salvation (or God in some sense) is at the top of the mountain, and we are all trying to reach it (or him) by our different routes. We will all get there in the end, even though our paths are different. In chapter four we shall have more to say about other religions, but on this point at least we need to be clear from the start.

Religions vary greatly in the different things they prescribe as a means to whatever they describe as salvation. And there are certainly some non-Christian religious traditions that have an awareness of a need for undeserved grace from whatever deity is worshiped and ask the deity for some help. But wherever the religious prescription is essentially a matter of human endeavor, the Bible cuts across all such efforts, for they are ultimately futile. Salvation belongs to God alone, and those to whom God freely gives it on the basis of what God himself has done. As for the metaphor of the mountain, the Bible would be more inclined to reverse it. Human beings are on many different paths *down* the mountain, fleeing from God and ever more distant from him in sin and rebellion. Religions in themselves are no answer to our deepest problems.

Salvation has God as its source, even when human agents are involved. In the Bible there are, of course, many instances when salvation comes through human agency. That is to say, human beings were involved in the process by which people were saved. But even then, either implicitly or sometimes quite explicitly, the *source* of the power to save still lies with

God. The book of Judges illustrates this principle again and again.

Gideon was told to go and deliver (or save—the word is the same in Hebrew) Israel. He would be the deliverer, but only because God would be with him.

> The LORD turned to him and said, "Go in the strength you have and save Israel out of Midian's hand. Am I not sending you?"
>
> "But Lord," Gideon asked, "how can I save Israel? My clan is the weakest in Manasseh, and I am the least in my family." (Judg 6:14-15)

But when Gideon assembled his army, it was systematically reduced in numbers before he could begin his campaign. The point of this process was explicitly to ensure that God would be seen to be the true source of the victory, not the size of the army.

> The LORD said to Gideon, "You have too many men for me to deliver Midian into their hands. In order that Israel may not boast against me that her own strength has saved her. . . .
>
> The LORD said to Gideon, "With the three hundred men that lapped I will save you and give the Midianites into your hands. Let all the other men go, each to his own place." (Judg 7:2, 7; contrast the ironic refusal of God to save them on another occasion in Judg 10:11-14)

Similarly, David's victory over Goliath would show the world who really is the God with power to save. David was the human agent of Israel's salvation on that occasion, but David himself was well aware of who the real savior was: "All those gathered here will know that it is not by sword or spear that the LORD saves; for the battle is the LORD's, and he will give all of you into our hands" (1 Sam 17:47).

God alone can save. The constantly repeated message of the Old Testament is that only Yahweh, the LORD God of Israel, can save. This is the message especially of the prophets. There may be many who claim to offer salvation, but they are all false.

Yahweh saves when nobody else can or does.

The LORD looked and was displeased
    that there was no justice.
He saw that there was no one,
    he was appalled that there was no one to intervene;
so his own arm worked salvation for him,
    and his own righteousness sustained him.
He put on righteousness as his breastplate,
    and the helmet of salvation on his head;
he put on the garments of vengeance
    and wrapped himself in zeal as in a cloak. (Is 59:15-17)

Astrologers cannot save.

All the counsel you have received has only worn you out!
    Let your astrologers come forward,
those stargazers who make predictions month by month,
    let them save you from what is coming upon you.
Surely they are like stubble;
    the fire will burn them up.
They cannot even save themselves
    from the power of the flame. (Is 47:13-14)

Kings, mere mortals that they are, cannot save.

Do not put your trust in princes,
    in mortal men, who cannot save. (Ps 146:3)

Military power cannot save.

No king is saved by the size of his army;
    no warrior escapes by his great strength.
A horse is a vain hope for deliverance;
    despite all its great strength it cannot save. (Ps 33:16-17)

Other gods are contemptibly unable to save.

"I, even I, am the LORD,
    and apart from me there is no savior.

I have revealed and saved and proclaimed—
    I, and not some foreign god among you.
You are my witnesses," declares the LORD, "that I am God.
    Yes, and from ancient days I am he.
No one can deliver out of my hand.
    When I act, who can reverse it?" (Is 43:11-13)

Gather together and come;
    assemble, you fugitives from the nations.
Ignorant are those who carry about idols of wood,
    who pray to gods that cannot save.
Declare what is to be, present it—
    let them take counsel together.
Who foretold this long ago,
    who declared it from the distant past?
Was it not I, the LORD?
    And there is no God apart from me,
a righteous God and a Savior;
    there is none but me. (Is 45:20-21)

We shall look at New Testament material in more depth later, but here is a point worth noticing right away. The Greek word for "savior" (*sōtēr*) is applied to God eight times in the New Testament and to Jesus sixteeen times, *but to nobody else at all ever.* And yet the term *sōtēr* was a fairly common term in the classical world. It was applied both to human kings and military deliverers, and also to the great gods and heroes of mythology. Lots of people in the ancient world of Greece and Rome could be easily described as saviors. But not in the New Testament. "Salvation belongs to our God . . . and to the Lamb." Nobody else deserves even the *vocabulary* of salvation, let alone the reality of it.

Since, then, only the God of the Bible can and does save, salvation is clearly not something you can *get* from any religion—considered as a set of human activities or aspirations. In the debate over religious pluralism, people sometimes ask the question, "Is there salvation in other religions?" But the form of the question itself is highly misleading. It embodies a hidden assumption that is biblically quite false. The assumption built into that question is that salvation is something you get from some religion or another. We assume we get salvation from our Christian religion, so the only question is whether other people can get salvation from other religions.

But, according to the Bible, religion saves nobody. God does. We are not saved because we are Christians and do all the Christian religious things. We are saved because God has acted, in Christ, to accomplish salvation for us, and then simply calls on us to trust him. Nothing religious that we do is the means or the cause of our salvation. Our Christianity is the response we make, in faith and life, to the saving acts of God. Salvation belongs to God. It is not manipulated out of him by our religious activity, as if somehow we could participate in saving ourselves.

"Self-salvation is not a typically biblical perspective," says Professor Gerald O'Collins,[1] with undue understatement. "Self-salvation" is not even a *remotely* biblical perspective! It is, rather, utterly contrary to all the Bible has to say about the only source of salvation—God alone. Salvation is the property of the God of the Bible.

SALVATION AS THE IDENTITY OF GOD

This God and no other. The song of the redeemed in Revelation 7:10 is very specific and particular. "Salvation belongs to *our* God," they sing. They are not merely saying that there is some kind of link between salvation and deity as an abstract transcendent concept. The witness of this vast crowd is not to say, "If you want salvation, get yourself a god; any god will do." No, they are claiming that salvation belongs to *our* God— to *this* God. It is *this* God, the God of the biblical revelation and redemption, Yahweh the God of Old Testament Israel, the God and Father of our Lord Jesus Christ, the God who is not ashamed to be called "our God." *This* is the God to whom salvation belongs. So we move on from the previous point, that salvation is the property of God, to the further point that salvation is the property of this very particular God—this God and no other.

In fact, what makes this God so particular and distinctive above all other claimed deities is precisely his saving ability and activity. His very nature is to save. And he has proved that in history. Let's look at two texts, one from the Old Testament and one from the New, which express this point very clearly. In both cases, the context is one of a historical act of salvation, and in both cases those who witnessed it are urged to know the truth about who the living and saving God is.

Deuteronomy 4:32-35, 39.

> Ask now about the former days, long before your time, from the day God created man on the earth; ask from one end of the heavens to the other. Has anything so great as this ever happened, or has anything like it ever been heard of? Has any other people heard the voice of God speaking out of fire, as you have, and lived? Has any god ever tried to take for himself one nation out of another nation, by testings, by miraculous signs and wonders, by war, by a mighty hand and an outstretched arm, or by great and awesome deeds, like all the things the LORD your God did for you in Egypt before your very eyes?
>
> You were shown these things so that you might know that the LORD is God; besides him there is no other. . . . Acknowledge and take to heart this day that the LORD is God in heaven above and on the earth below. There is no other.

Moses recalls the great events in Old Testament Israel's history so far:

- God's revelation at Mount Sinai (Deut 4:33)
- God's redemption through the exodus (Deut 4:34)

Nothing like these things had ever happened in any other nation's history. God's salvation, as experienced by Old Testament Israel up to that point, was unprecedented (he had not done this at any other time) and unparalleled (he had not done it for any other people anywhere else). So, says Moses, this unique historical experience of Israel proves something about their unique God. The Israelites, Moses insists, now know exactly who the true and living God is. They know his identity—Yahweh, their God. All this historical experience was not merely so that they should know that there is only one God (formal monotheism). That would be true, but as James said, just believing in one God does not get you much further than the devils who also believe that. No, the point was, the Israelites now know the *identity* of God. They know *who* God is. The living God is the God who has revealed himself as Yahweh, and who has decisively acted in their history within living memory. So they must know Yahweh, and only Yahweh, as their unique saving God (Deut 4:35, 39).

Acts 4:8-12.

> Then Peter, filled with the Holy Spirit, said to them: "Rulers and elders of the people! If we are being called to account today for an act of kindness shown to a cripple and are asked how he was healed, then know this, you and all the people of Israel: It is by the name of Jesus Christ of Nazareth, whom you crucified but whom God raised from the dead, that this man stands before you healed. He is 'the stone you builders rejected, which has become the capstone.' Salvation is found in no one else, for there is no other name under heaven given to men by which we must be saved."

The interesting comparison here with the passage in Deuteronomy is that in both cases the speaker appeals to something that had happened, something that nobody could deny. In fact, in Acts 4:4-16, the authorities to whom Peter was speaking knew perfectly well that they could not deny what everybody in Jerusalem could see—a man crippled for years running and jumping around! So Peter builds his case about the resurrection of Jesus on that foundation: the crowds were witnesses of a healing; the apostles were witnesses of the resurrection. "You've seen a man healed; we've seen a man raised!"

And on that foundation he then goes on to make the astounding claim that salvation is now to be found in Jesus alone. Remember, these were Jews. They were already fully convinced from their Scriptures that salvation was an act of Yahweh alone—the God of Old Testament Israel. This God, says Peter, has now invested the uniqueness of his saving power in the unique person of the risen Jesus—and in nobody else: "Salvation is found in no one else [than Jesus], for there is no other name under heaven given to men by which we must be saved" (Acts 4:12). "No other God than Yahweh," says Moses. "No other name than Jesus," says Peter.

So we see that God's great saving acts, whether in the Old or New Testament, demonstrate the identity of the true and living God as the one and only source of salvation. Salvation is the work of *this* one God, revealed as Yahweh in the Old Testament, incarnated as Jesus of Nazareth in the Gospels. There is no other.

This is why the Bible lays such importance on *knowing God*. This is not just a matter of knowing that some god exists—i.e., having a general belief in God. Nor is it just a matter of knowing truths or statements about God—even if they are biblical and true. Rather it is a matter of knowing who God is, or who truly is God. The true God has proved his identity supremely through his power to save. The Israelites were to know Yahweh alone because Yahweh alone had saved them. "I am the LORD your God, who brought you out of Egypt. You shall acknowledge [*know*] no God but me, no Savior except me" (Hos 13:4). And in the same way, we now come to such saving knowledge of God through Jesus: "This is eternal life [which in John is synonymous with salvation]: that they may *know* you, the only true God, and Jesus Christ, whom you have sent" (Jn 17:3). Biblical salvation comes from encountering the biblical God.

I lived and taught in India for a number of years. On one occasion I was teaching a seminar over a weekend for Christian professionals in Andhra Pradesh, on one of my favorite themes—the ethical teaching of the Old Testament and how it applies to Christian living today. After the first session a man came to speak to me, his eyes gleaming. "I'm so glad you are teaching us from the Old Testament," he said, "for I became a Christian through reading the Old Testament." Now you don't often hear that, as an Old Testament teacher, so I asked him to tell me his story.

He was then a lecturer in engineering at the local university. But he had grown up among the despised Dalit (outcaste) community in his village, and his whole family had suffered greatly at the hands of the high-caste Hindus in the village—all kinds of harassment, violence and injustice. He had a great thirst for revenge, and so he worked very hard at school, to get to university, so that he could get a job with some influence and power, and then turn the tables on his enemies. That, he said, was his deliberate intention.

The day he arrived at the university, he found a Bible on his bed in his room in the student hostel. It was in Telugu (his state language), and it had been left there by some Christian students of the Union of Evangelical Students of India. He had never read one before, though he knew that it was the Christians' holy book. He opened it at random and started reading the story of Naboth and Ahab in 1 Kings 21. He was amazed. The story had so many familiar elements. "This was my story," he said. His family had also experienced theft of land, false accusations, murders, the brutality of the powerful against the ordinary people.

But then he read on and was amazed to read about another man called Elijah, who, in the name of some God called Yahweh (or whatever the translation of the personal name of the God of Old Testament Israel is in the Telugu Bible), denounced King Ahab, and said that he would be judged and punished by this God. This was astounding, my friend said. Here was a god who took the side of the suffering ones and *condemned the government* and the powerful for their wicked deeds. *"I never knew such a god existed"* were his exact words to me, which I have never forgotten.

My friend had millions of gods within Hinduism to choose from. He knew the names of many gods. But he had never heard of such a god as he was reading about in this Bible. Here was a god quite unlike anything he had met before in his own religion.

So he went back to the beginning of the book and started reading the Bible through from Genesis. He grew even more amazed. "This god thinks of everything!" he said, as he read through the laws of Exodus, Leviticus and Deuteronomy. He was impressed by the character of the God of Israel, with his concern for the poor and needy, his passion for justice, and so on. Exactly the kind of god he was looking for in his own thirst for justice.

When he reached Isaiah and started to read of the love of God (in Is 43, for example), he was not so pleased, he told me, for he wanted a god who would give him vengeance on his oppressors, not love them! However, just about that time, the Christian students visited him, and like Philip in Acts 8, led him from the text of Isaiah to Jesus, and eventually led him to faith and conversion.

What struck me in this man's testimony was this. It was precisely the *story* of the Old Testament that demonstrated the *identity* of the God of the Bible. Furthermore, he found great surprise, but also great reassurance, in aspects of the identity and character of the Old Testament God that some Christians find disturbing. But essentially he found salvation not because he found "a god" (for he had plenty of gods already), but because he learned the true identity of the true and living God, through his encounter with the text of the Bible.

Yahweh is salvation. What we have seen so far is that salvation defines the particularity and uniqueness of this God—the God revealed as Yahweh and known to us through Jesus. But the Bible goes even further than this and defines the very *identity* of God in terms of salvation. Saving is one of the most dominant activities and characteristics of this biblical God. It is so distinctively typical of him that sometimes Old Testament writers could simply say, "Yahweh *is* salvation."

One of the earliest poetic celebrations of salvation in the Bible comes immediately in the wake of the crossing of the sea at the exodus. In it, Moses sings,

> The LORD is my strength and my song;
>   he has become my salvation. (Ex 15:2)

Among the oldest metaphors for Yahweh in early Hebrew poetry is that which describes him as "the Rock" of Israel's salvation (Deut 32:15). Yahweh is portrayed as Israel's Savior God from the very beginning of their history.

In the book of Psalms Yahweh is above all else the God who saves. That is who he is and that is what he does most consistently, most often and best. The Hebrew root *yaša'* (to save) occurs 136 times in Psalms and this accounts for 40 percent of all the uses of that word in the whole Old Testament. Yahweh is

- the God of my salvation, or God my Savior (Ps 18:46; 25:5; 51:14, etc.)
- the horn of my salvation (Ps 18:2)
- the Rock of my salvation (Ps 89:26; 95:1)
- my salvation and my honor (Ps 62:6-7)
- my Savior and my God (Ps 42:5)

And Yahweh is not just *"my* savior," and not even only the savior of *humans,* for this God saves "both man and beast" (Ps 36:6). Israelite worship and teaching constantly linked Yahweh with salvation. No wonder that when it was necessary to restore the faith of the people of Israel in their great God at the time of their lowest ebb in exile, the word from Isaiah reminded them of this great heritage of worship by presenting God in these terms, echoing so many psalms:

I am the LORD, your God,
    the Holy One of Israel, your Savior. (Is 43:3)

When we move to the New Testament, we immediately find the angel instructing Joseph to call Mary's son Jehoshua (Joshua, Jeshua—or in its Greek form, Jesus), for "he will save his people from their sins" (Mt 1:21). The name itself literally means, *"Yahweh is salvation."* This will be the name by which God will be known to the ends of the earth, by those who love, honor, worship and proclaim the name of Jesus. As millions of believers bow at the name of Jesus, they simultaneously declare God to be the saving God of the Bible.

Luke gives us the wonderful picture of the aged Simeon meeting Jesus face to face as a baby. He had been told that he would not die before he had seen "the Lord's Christ." Then one day, he was able to hold the infant Jesus in his arms. Most likely he asked Joseph and Mary the name of their baby, and when they told him, he burst into praise and thanked God that now "my eyes have seen *your salvation*"—your Jehoshua (Lk 2:30). God's salvation was snuggling in his arms! The identity of God, the mission of God, the action of God, were all bound up in that one name.

Paul, a Jew who had celebrated the God of Israel as Savior all his life, now links that great pillar of his faith with the name and work of Jesus—again and again. The most astonishing concentration of salvation language comes in the tiny letter to Titus. There, in the space of three short chapters, Paul piles up the phrases "God our Savior" and "Christ our Savior" seven times.

The God revealed as Yahweh in the Old Testament, and in Jesus of Nazareth in the New Testament, is above all else the God who saves. That is the distinctive mark of his uniqueness and the defining mark of his identity.

Other gods cannot save. In sharp contrast, other gods are distinguished from Yahweh most commonly by the fact that they cannot save. We saw above that only Yahweh can save, as against all other claimaints—including humans like kings or armies. But the contrast between Yahweh and all other *gods* is especially clear. They are simply impotent in this key department of deity. False gods are as much identifiable by their proven inability to save as the living God is identifiable by his proven power to do so. This is the essential contrast between false gods and the one true living God. The God of Israel can and does save those who call on him. All other gods can't and don't.

In fact, those false so-called gods can't even save themselves.

The early encounters between Yahweh and Baal in the book of Judges present this stark contrast sometimes with comic intent. For example, you remember how, in Judges 6, Gideon broke down the altar of Baal in his village (but by night, for fear of his family). When the deed is discovered, the crowd comes to arrest Gideon, but his father stands in their way to protect his son. Gideon's father's reply to the mob is wonderfully sarcastic.

> But Joash replied to the hostile crowd around him, "Are you going to plead Baal's cause? Are you trying to *save* him? Whoever fights for him shall be put to death by morning! If Baal really is a god, he can defend himself when someone breaks down his altar." (Judg 6:31, my italics)

If Baal really is a *god,* ought he not to be able to save his own altar? Or is he so weak that he actually needs this mob to save him? What kind of god needs to be saved by humans when the whole point of being a god (one would think) is to be able to save your worshipers? Are we missing something here, citizens?

Similar sarcasm and scorn are poured on the great imperial gods of Babylon at a much later stage of Israel's Old Testament history.

> Bel bows down, Nebo stoops low;
>   their idols are borne by beasts of burden.
> The images that are carried about are burdensome,
>   a burden for the weary.
> They stoop and bow down together;
>   unable to rescue the burden,
>   they themselves go off into captivity. (Is 46:1-7)

The prophet foresees Babylon being attacked and its people fleeing for safety. Bel and Nebo, gods of Babylon, are caricatured as stooping down from their heavenly residence because their idols are being carted off by their worshipers. The worshipers are struggling under the burden as they flee from their fallen city. Indeed, they have to load their gods onto ox carts! What kind of god is it that cannot save even its own idol, let alone its worshipers? What strange reversal is it that makes the worshipers find that their god is now a burden *they have to carry,* rather than

a strong champion who will *carry them* in their hour of need (as Israel's
God had done from the dawn of their history; see Is 46:3-4)? No, the
very nature of such a false god is that "though one cries out to it, it does
not answer; *it cannot save*" (Is 46:7). Saving people is the one thing false
gods can't do.

This is as true at the individual, domestic level as it is in grand imperial politics. The deluded worshiper of an idol seems blinded to the sham
and impotence of the god he has created for himself as a byproduct of
heating and eating. He calls to it for salvation, but that is the one thing
it cannot ever deliver (Is 44:9-20).

> Half of the wood he burns in the fire;
>> over it he prepares his meal,
>> he roasts his meat and eats his fill.
> He also warms himself and says,
>> "Ah! I am warm; I see the fire."
> From the rest he makes a god, his idol;
>> he bows down to it and worships.
> He prays to it and says,
>> "*Save* me; you are my god." . . .
> He feeds on ashes, a deluded heart misleads him;
>> he cannot *save* himself, or say,
>> "Is not this thing in my right hand a lie?" (Is 44:16-17, 20, my italics)

Jeremiah, similarly, mocked those who had abandoned the living God
for all kinds of idolatries. But then, when they discovered that all their
gods failed them and could not deliver the salvation they wanted, they
start pleading with God again—only to meet a very sobering response:

> They say to wood, "You are my father,"
>> and to stone, "You gave me birth."
> They have turned their backs to me
>> and not their faces;
>> yet when they are in trouble, they say,

"Come and save us!"
Where then are the gods you made for yourselves?
    Let them come if they can save you
    when you are in trouble!
For you have as many gods
    as you have towns, O Judah. (Jer 2:27-28)

False gods never fail to fail.

The trouble is, we never fail to forget this fact. We still look for salvation from saviors that are anything or anyone but the living, saving God. Although as Christians we use the language of salvation in our distinctly "religious" way, people in the secular world still also use it, sometimes in frivolous ways, and sometimes more seriously.

During the 2002 World Cup, posters were displayed in some shops in London with a photo of David Beckham, arms stretched out wide, set against a background of the red cross of St. George, the flag of England. Underneath this image, with its obvious and rather blasphemous echoes of the crucifixion, was the caption, "Beckham, our saviour."

Time magazine, March 4, 2002, had as its cover a photo of the rock singer Bono, of U2, with the headline, "Can Bono save the world?" The reference was to his very public mission of compassion and justice for the world's poor. Bono uses his celebrity status to enormously positive ends, in the cause of international justice. But his efforts hardly qualify as "saving the world."

More cynically, the British press once mocked Prime Minister Tony Blair's rapid tour of several African countries, describing it as his mission of "saving Africa"—and obviously suggesting that even he had no hope of achieving that in a few short days in a few capital cities.

So the language of saving and saviors is still out there. But all such human or idolized forms of salvation can never deliver what they promise—even when what they promise is good in itself. Salvation belongs to our God. All other sources or claims are ultimately flawed, inadequate and disillusioning.

QUESTIONS FOR REFLECTION OR DISCUSSION

1. Salvation belongs to God; it is God's property. What does this say to some popular forms of mission and evangelism in which the gospel is "marketed" as though salvation were a product that we can "sell" to people? What are the results of such human-centered techniques?

2. This chapter stressed the importance of knowing the true identity and character of the biblical God. What aspects of God as seen in the Bible stand in greatest contrast to the culture that surrounds you in your local context?

3. "False gods never fail to fail." What are the false gods in your local context, and what is the evidence of their popularity? In what ways do people look for "salvation" from them? And in what ways do those gods fail to deliver?

3

Salvation and God's Covenant Blessing

"SALVATION BELONGS TO OUR GOD." IN CHAPTER TWO we thought about those last two words in relation to the identity of God. We need to know who God is before we talk about any kind of salvation. Salvation is the property of this very particular God, known through his revelation in the Bible, with the personal name Yahweh in the Old Testament, and his incarnation in Jesus of Nazareth.

But the expression "our God" had even more significance than that for biblical people. It was an essential part of Old Testament Israel's *covenant* faith. So, just as in chapter two we were thinking of the *theocentric* dimension, here we are thinking of the *covenantal* dimension of biblical salvation. God had called the people of Israel into a relationship with himself. It was a relationship that included what God had done (he had chosen, called and redeemed them, and he continued to protect and provide for them) and what the people of Israel were to do in response (to love and worship Yahweh alone, and to obey him fully). So, reciprocally, Yahweh would be known as the God of Israel. And Israel would be known as the people of Yahweh. This was the covenant relationship in the Old Testament.

The phrase *Yhwh 'ĕlōhênû*, "The LORD *our God*," is the commonest way of summing up Israel's covenantal faith in the Old Testament: "You have declared this day that the LORD is your God. . . . And the LORD has declared this day that you are his people" (Deut 26:17-18).

The clearest definition of Israel's creed is the Shema: "Hear, O Israel: the LORD *our God*, the LORD is one. Love the LORD your God with all your heart and with all your soul and with all your strength" (Deut 6:4-5).

So when Revelation tells us that the great crowd was singing '"Salvation belongs to *our God,"* it is a clear echo of this covenantal language. Salvation, then, belongs to the covenantal God—not just to this *God,* but to the God of *this people* and their history. Biblical salvation has to be understood in the context of God's covenantal relationship to his people, Old and New Testament. Salvation in the Bible is not something just dropped from heaven as a timeless benefit. It is rooted in the story of the Bible, and particularly in the story of the covenant relationship between God and his people—which began right back in the Old Testament.

We shall study this covenantal aspect of biblical salvation in chapters three and four. Here in chapter three we shall think about the *blessing* that is such an integral part of salvation within the covenant. What exactly does the Bible mean when it talks about the blessings of salvation? And in chapter four we shall think about the *story* that runs through the whole Bible as the story of God's covenant. For within that story we shall see that salvation is described in terms of the past, the present and the future. These three dimensions of salvation are fundamental to a full biblical grasp of what salvation means.

ABRAHAMIC BLESSING

Abraham in context. We begin, then, with blessing, and that takes us back to Abraham. Strictly speaking, it takes us back even further. Blessing was built into creation itself, of course (as we shall explore below), but then it was gravely threatened by human sin and rebellion. But even in the context of the Fall and God's declared judgment on humanity, God had promised that the seed of the woman would crush the head of the serpent (Gen 3:15). That is to say, a human descendant of Adam and Eve would eventually win the victory over Satan.

This promise in Genesis 3:15 is often called the *protevangelium*—that is, the first announcement of the good news, which is later filled out in the whole biblical gospel and accomplished by Jesus Christ. This verse certainly gives hope that God's blessing had not been utterly terminated by the Fall. The word of judgment was not God's final word. There would be hope and victory in the future. But it is with the call of Abraham and God's promise to him that we see the beginning of the implementation of that initial promise in Genesis 3:15. This will be the route by which God's redemptive blessing will come to the nations.

God's covenant with Abraham is recorded in Genesis 12:1-3, but it is utterly crucial to read it against the backdrop of Genesis 3–11. Human sin and rebellion had been escalating from its first instance in Genesis 3, through family violence and social corruption. The climax was the great failed attempt at self-salvation, the tower of Babel (Gen 11). The world had become a place in which the human race now lived in division and strife upon an earth that strains under God's curse. What can God possibly do about the problem posed by the nations of humanity living in such conditions? The historical answer, in line with the promise of Genesis 3:15, begins in Genesis 12 and runs right on to Revelation 22.

The rest of the Bible is God's answer to the brokenness of the world because of human sin. You could think of the Bible as a whole in this way: *Genesis 1–11 sets the question to which Genesis 12–Revelation 22 is the answer.* It is the story of the triumph of blessing over curse.

God initiated a redemptive covenant of blessing—a plan of salvation that would lead to Christ and eventually find fulfillment in the redeemed humanity from every nation, whom we see in Revelation 7. God chose and called Abram and Sarai, and made the remarkable promise to them, in which *blessing* is the key word.

The LORD said to Abram, "Get up and go from your country, your people and your father's household and go to the land I will show you.

"I will make you into a great nation
  and I will bless you;
I will make your name great,
  and be a blessing.
I will bless those who bless you,
  and the one who curses you I will curse;
and through you all peoples on earth will be blessed." (Gen 12:1-3,
my translation)

The nation that would come from Abraham, then, would be a people who would know the saving blessing of God. God's salvation entered human history through a community. Starting from one man, this would become a large family by the end of Genesis, then a whole nation by the beginning of Exodus—the nation of Old Testament Israel. This nation would experience God's salvation and God's blessing. What they would do (and fail to do) in response is another matter, but this was unquestionably the unique experience into which God called them.

One chosen for the sake of all. But the Abrahamic covenant makes the further promise of blessing to *all the nations*. Indeed, this is the climactic bottom line of the Abrahamic covenant—textually and theologically: "through you all the families/nations of the earth will find blessing." This universal vista that is intrinsic to the Abrahamic covenant is central to our biblical understanding of salvation—indeed to our whole Christian understanding of the gospel and of mission. The man (Abraham) who would become a family, and then a nation (Old Testament Israel), would, through Christ, eventually become the father of people from all nations (spiritually) in a multinational community that now does indeed span the whole earth.

The unique covenant relationship between the people of Old Testament Israel and their saving, covenantal God would be precisely for the sake of the *other* nations who did not yet know God in that way. The election and salvation of Old Testament Israel was ultimately for the blessing of all nations. Salvation meant blessing *on* a particular people (Israel) and blessing *through* that particular people (for all nations). God chose to bless *this* people in order to bless *all* peoples. We must hold together this double affirmation of particularity and universality, for both are clearly taught in the Bible.

The salvation of Israel (in Old Testament terms) was never meant to be exclusively for her benefit alone, but part of a historical process within which God planned to bring salvation to all nations. We must never allow the Old Testament's emphasis on the unique and distinctive nature of Israel as God's holy and elect people to become a matter of exclusive privilege, as if they were the favorites of God, or the only ones he cared about. On the contrary, the Old Testament Israelites were chosen by God, yes, but chosen as one chooses an instrument for an important task—chosen to be the historical vehicle for his saving purpose, through Christ, for all nations. Far from being God's favorites, they were all the more exposed to the severity of God's judgment (as Amos 3:2 and many other prophets made clear).

A world of nations. We can understand this point further by looking again at the context of Genesis 12. It follows not only the story of the tower of Babel in Genesis 11, but also the table of nations in Genesis 10. After the flood (Gen 6–9), God had renewed his mandate to the human race to be fruitful and multiply and fill the earth. Genesis 10 describes the spreading of the nations across the face of the earth in fulfillment of that command. Genesis 11 describes an attempted halt in that process, with the decision to settle in one place and build a tower for security and "a great name." God frustrates that arrogant early totalitarian experiment, and the scattering of the nations resumes, but in conditions of confusion and dividedness.

The ethnic diversity of Genesis 10, however, is seen as a good thing in itself. God *intends* humanity to enjoy its ethnic, cultural and linguistic diversity. These things are not only part of creation (cf. Acts 17:26); they will also remain as part of our redeemed condition in the new creation (cf. Rev 5:9; 21:24; 22:2). So the universal purpose for which God called Abraham in Genesis 12:3 is in itself an echo of the universal intention apparent already in Genesis 10. The call of Old Testament Israel inherent in Genesis 12 is for the sake of the nations already seen in Genesis 10.

One could put it like this: Genesis 10 and 11 together portray both the *fact* of the world of nations (in Genesis 10) and the *problem* of the nations (in Genesis 11); Genesis 12 portrays the beginning of the *redemption* of the nations. God works on the global stage. The global world of Genesis 10 will be seen again, magnified almost beyond recognition, in the global world of Revelation. The particular world of Old Testament Israel, though it dominates the story that follows until the coming of Christ, is only an instrumental staging post along the way in that grand universal narrative.

So whatever nation, tribe, people or language you may belong to, as a reader of this Global Christian Library, you are implicitly included in *both* sides of the story so far. You are included in the global *creational perspective* of Genesis 10 (the many nations that fill the face of the earth), and you are included in the global *redemptive scope* of Genesis 12:3 (the "all nations" whom God promised to bless). And if you are in Christ, then you will join those who, in fulfillment of God's promise to Abraham, will be there in the redeemed humanity from all nations, praising God in the new creation according to Revelation. These are great and heart-warming biblical truths. Such wonderful biblical doctrine should fill our hearts with amazement and praise.

Now it should be no surprise to any Christian reader that we are talking about *salvation* and *blessing* in the same breath. We easily talk about "the blessings of our salvation." We quickly remember the wonderful opening words of Paul's letter to the Ephesians, with which he introduces his soaring description of God's work of salvation in the rest of Ephesians 1: "Blessed be the God and Father of our Lord Jesus Christ, who has blessed us in Christ with every spiritual blessing in the heavenly places" (Eph 1:3 NRSV).

But we need to resist the tendency, therefore, to think that only spiritual blessings count as real blessings, or that salvation is exclusively a matter of spiritual blessings. Of course we know clearly from the Bible as a whole that there are dimensions of salvation that can only be described in spiritual terms—God's forgiveness, being born again, being justified by grace through faith, being indwelt by Christ through his Spirit, etc. But it is important to allow the *whole* Bible to shape our *whole* theology. And in this case, since we are seeking an understanding of salvation from the whole Bible, we must include all that it has to say about God's blessing.

Let us then build up our understanding around several key aspects of blessing that we find in the Old Testament, which are not lost or canceled out in the New Testament. Rather, these Old Testament dimensions of blessing are taken up and included within that total blessing of salvation that is ours in Christ. And that means starting right back in Genesis. So we return to our key text in this chapter—Genesis 12:1-3.[1]

There can be no mistaking what the central theme of Genesis 12:1-3 is. The words *bless* and *blessing* gleam like jewels. The Hebrew root *brk,* as a verb or a noun, occurs five times in these three verses. God declares

- that he will *bless* Abraham
- that Abraham is to be a *blessing*
- that God will *bless* those who *bless* Abraham
- that all families on earth will count themselves *blessed* through him[2]

The God whose blessing first bathed creation is on the move to bless yet again, with repetitive intensity and startling extent. But what exactly do the words mean? What might an attentive reader of Scripture understand by *blessing* here?

To answer that question we must properly begin in the immediate environment of our text—the book of Genesis—and then move forward to see how it gathers weight and significance through the Bible. So we need to start right at the beginning and notice how the opening chapters of the Bible are rich in the language of blessing.

BLESSING IS CREATIONAL AND RELATIONAL

The creational aspect. The first creatures to be blessed by God were fish and birds. In the majestic account of creation in Genesis 1, God's blessing is pronounced three times: on day five he blessed these creatures of the sea and air; then on day six he blessed human beings; and finally on day seven he blessed the Sabbath. The first two blessings are immediately followed by the instruction to multiply and fill the seas and the earth. The third blessing is followed by the words of sanctification and rest that define the Sabbath. *Blessing,* then, in this foundational creation account at the very beginning of our Bible, is constituted by fruitfulness, abundance and fullness on the one hand and by enjoying rest within creation in holy and harmonious relationship with our Creator God on the other. Blessing is off to a good start.

The next time we hear of God's blessing, it is launching the new world after the flood, and the language is almost the same as in the first creation account (Genesis 9). God blesses Noah and his family, and instructs them to be fruitful, multiply and fill the earth. At the same time, God enters into a relationship with them which includes respect for life—whether animal or human blood—and the preservation of life. These blessings and commands are then worked out in the spreading of the nations in Genesis 10.

So when we come to Genesis 12:1-3, the word of blessing must, from the context so far, include at least the concept of fruitfulness, multiplication, spreading, filling and abundance. As we read on in Genesis, this creational content of blessing predominates. In fact, the root *brk*, as a verb or a noun, occurs eighty-eight times in Genesis, which is just over a fifth of all its occurrences in the whole Old Testament. When God blesses someone, it normally includes increase of family or flocks or wealth or all three. God's blessing means enjoying the good gifts of God's creation in abundance.

God's blessing is manifested most obviously in human prosperity and well-being; long life, wealth, peace, good harvests and children are the items that figure most frequently in lists of blessings such as in Genesis 24:35-36, Leviticus 26:4-13 and Deuteronomy 28:3-15. What modern secular man calls luck or success the Old Testament calls blessing, for it insists that God alone is the source of all good fortune. Indeed, the presence of God walking among his people is the highest of his blessings (Lev 26:11-12). Material blessings are in themselves tangible expressions of divine benevolence. Blessing not only connects the patriarchal narratives with each other (cf. Gen 24:1; 26:3; 35:9; 39:5); it also links them with the primeval history (cf. Gen 1:28; 5:2; 9:1). *The promises of blessing to the patriarchs are thus a reassertion of God's original intentions for man.*[3]

Blessing, not necessarily prosperity. That final sentence is very important. Blessing is God's original intention for human life on earth. The goodness of creation and the goodness of enjoying creation are central truths of the Bible. God wants his human creatures to enjoy the blessing of their creatureliness—all the blessings that God built into creation itself. But this has to be put in a properly balanced context if we are to avoid the kind of perversion and distortion of this biblical teaching that is preached in prosperity theology.

It is one thing to affirm gladly that God can and does bless people in a material way, with fulfillment of life, fruitfulness in their families and enjoyment of the good things of creation. But it is another thing altogether to insist that we have an *entitlement* to all such things or that if we do not receive them in abundance, then either God has not blessed us or we are lacking in faith.

Of course it is true that God does not want his human creatures (whether Christian or not) to live in destitution and need. And it is also true that people who do live in such circumstances justly long for relief from their suffering. But unfortunately prosperity theology tends to go way beyond any proper biblical concern for justice (and rarely to my knowledge do the preachers of prosperity ever get involved in the political and economic struggle for justice or addressing the causes of poverty).

Instead this teaching seems to pander very much to our fallen human tendency toward greed and selfishness. It's not just that people justifiably want escape from poverty. People are enticed to want more and more of all the material wealth they can get their hands on—and as fast as possible, through a miracle. And so they are led to seize on biblical verses, out of context, that seem to promise such miracles, in exchange for faith or sizeable money gifts to whomever is doing the preaching. Such teaching is a distortion of God's blessing in relation to material things, in the same way that corrupt sexual lust is a distortion of God's blessing in relation to our sexuality. The proper response to this kind of distortion is not to deny the good thing itself while condemning the abuse of it.

To follow up my comparison, the Bible clearly teaches that human sexuality was God's own idea and creational design, intended for our good and our blessing. But we also know that because we are all fallen, our sexual nature is corrupted by lust, power and greed. Many people abuse themselves and others through promiscuity and all the exploitation of sex that we see around us. But the answer to such fallen *abuse* of sex is not to fall into the opposite error and regard *sex in itself* as something dirty and sinful. Our sexual complementarity is part of God's good creation, and he wants us to enjoy it to the full, within the proper context that he created for it, namely monogamous, heterosexual, non-incestuous marriage (Gen 2:24). Such proper enjoyment of sex is part of God's creational blessing, and it is for us to receive it with thanks and joy (as Adam did when receiving Eve). Enjoyment of sex as a creational blessing is right and good, provided it is within the context that God created for it. Exploitation of sex for promiscuous gratification is wrong and sinful.

Similarly, we know that because we are all fallen, our use of material things is corrupted by greed and selfishness, by the love of money and all the sins of covetousness, theft, exploitation, injustice and excessive affluence. Under a veneer of religious language and spurious biblical quotation, prosperity theology panders to exactly these tendencies in us. If I can get rich quick by some religious activity and by just "claiming my miracle," why waste time and effort in working for it? Or even more demanding, by working for the alleviation of other people's poverty? But the answer to such false teaching is not to fall into the opposite error and regard the material world and its natural goods and pleasures as something wicked and sinful. Asceticism (withdrawal from all physical or material enjoyment) for the wrong reason is no better than sexual celibacy for the wrong reason—the wrong reason being a rejection of something that is good in itself as though it were evil (see 1 Tim 4:1-5, balanced by 1 Tim 5:3-10).

The physical world is God's creation, and God wants us to enjoy it under his blessing, by using and sharing it with care, justice, compassion and generosity. Of course God can bless people in all kinds of other ways, including blessing those who for many reasons lack the fullness of earth's good things. But we should not despise or reject what the Bible itself affirms many times: the good gifts of creation are part of the blessing of God, which he intends us to enjoy.

The relational aspect. However, there is nothing mechanical about this. Blessing is set within relationship. And that *relational* element is both vertical and horizontal. That is, blessing is set in the context of relationship with God, and it is something to be shared in relationship with other human beings.

On the one hand, *vertically,* those who are blessed know the God who is blessing them, and seek to live in faithful relationship with their God. When we look at the personal religious faith and practice of the ancestral families of Israel in Genesis, we see that it included sincere worship, building of altars, prayer, trust, obedience and (in the case of Abraham at least) a deepening personal intimacy with God.

Even outsiders like Abimelech knew that it was Yahweh who was blessing his strange neighbors (Gen 26:29). Indeed, the patriarchs normally do not hesitate to witness concerning the God who has blessed them. They openly attribute the good things they enjoy to the blessing of Yahweh.

Theirs is not a mute faith. The patriarchs verbalize to others the reality of Yahweh that they have experienced in their lives: they tell of his provision of wealth ([Gen] 30:30; 31:5-13; 33:10-11; cf. 24:35); his protection and guidance ([Gen] 31:42; 50:20; cf. 24:40-49, 56); his giving of children ([Gen] 33:5); . . . and their commitment to his moral standards ([Gen] 39:9).[4]

Living in that relationship with God was never easy, though. For Abraham, God's final sworn confirmation of blessing comes only after the most severe testing imaginable (Gen 22). And the mysterious account of Jacob wrestling with God ends with Jacob eliciting a blessing through a bruising face-to-face encounter (Gen 32:26-29).

But whatever the circumstances, the patriarchs were very conscious of the source of the blessing that had accompanied them all through life. They knew that their blessings were all wrapped up with their relationship with God. When blind and aged Jacob blesses the two sons of Joseph, he acknowledges that the blessing he now passes on is one that has attended his own life like a shepherd protecting a wandering and vulnerable sheep, and one that had marked the life of his father and grandfather as they walked before God. These are very beautiful words, showing very clearly that Jacob knew from whom his blessing had come:

> May the God before whom my fathers
> Abraham and Isaac walked,
> the God who has been my shepherd
> all my life to this day,
> the Angel who has delivered me from all harm
> —may he bless these boys. (Gen 48:15-16)

On the other hand, *horizontally,* the relational element of blessing reaches out to those around. Genesis has several instances of other people being blessed through contact with those whom God has blessed. Those who inherit the Abrahamic family blessing are then found to fulfill God's purpose that they should be a blessing to others:

- Laban is enriched by God's blessing on Jacob (Gen 30:27-30).
- Potiphar is blessed through the presence of Joseph (Gen 39:5).
- Pharaoh is blessed by Jacob (Gen 47:7, 10).

The one remarkable exception to this (to which Hebrews gives considerable theological significance) is the moment when Abraham himself is blessed by Melchizedek, rather than the other way round (Gen 14:18-20; cf. Heb. 7).

The most beautiful combination of the creational and relational dimensions of blessing is found in Jacob's blessing on Joseph. Read these rich words of Jacob's blessing and observe how it holds together three dimensions: first, the source of all blessing—God; second, the personal and covenantal relationship within which that blessing is enjoyed (he is "your father's God," "the Rock of Israel," etc); and, third, the creational abundance which the blessing envisages.

> Because of the hand of the Mighty One of Jacob,
>   because of the Shepherd, the Rock of Israel,
> because of your father's God, who helps you,
>   because of the Almighty who blesses you
> with blessings of the heavens above,
>   blessings of the deep that lies below,
>   blessings of the breast and the womb.
> Your father's blessings are greater
>   than the blessings of the ancient mountains,
>   than the bounty of the age-old hills.
> Let all these rest on the head of Joseph. (Gen 49:24-26)

BLESSING IS MISSIONAL AND HISTORICAL

Missional. *"Go . . . and be a blessing."* The words that launch both halves of God's address to Abraham in Genesis 12:1-3 are both, in fact, imperatives (though the second is often translated as expressing a sequence, or result—"and you will be a blessing"; but it is a command in Hebrew).

So the combined force is to entrust Abraham with a mission. Provided Abraham will obey God, then not only will God fulfill his promises *to* Abraham, but also God will fulfill the mission he has *through* Abraham— to bless all nations through him and his descendants. Abraham must leave his own land so that blessing will come to peoples of all lands.

Now clearly, *blessing* is here being presented as a command, as a task, as a role, within the framework of a promise. And this is something that goes beyond the sense of creational abundance that we have seen so far in Genesis. Abraham is not just going to "be blessed" (which is creational language). Rather he must *"be a blessing,"* and this entails a purpose and goal that stretches into the future. It is, in short, missional. Abraham and his descendants will be the agent of the mission of God. God intends to bless other people through Abraham and his descendants.

In fact, what we have here in Genesis 12:1-3 is the launch of God's *redemptive* mission. This is the opening act of God's great mission to restore what humanity seemed intent on wrecking, and to save humanity itself from the consequences of our own wicked folly. In other words, this is the start of salvation history. But it is expressed in terms of *blessing*. The repeated use of this word *blessing* links the story of Abraham with the creation narratives that precede it. God's work of redemption will take place within and for the created order, not in some other heavenly or mythological realm beyond it or to which we hope to escape.

It is creation that is broken by human sin, so it is creation and humanity together that God intends to mend. Ultimately, God's salvation is the restoration of God's blessing to creation and humanity. Salvation does not mean rescuing people *out of* creation to some other realm, but bringing back God's blessing *into* creation, through God's redeeming and transforming power. Salvation, then, is God's mission of redemptive blessing, restoring his whole creation to what was lost because of human sin and rebellion.

And since it was by human hands that sin and evil invaded life on earth, it would be by human means that God would act to redress it. God had promised that it would be the seed of Eve (i.e., a human being) that would crush the head of the serpent and thereby destroy his deleterious handiwork (Gen 3:15—the so-called protevangelium that we spoke of earlier). Attentive readers of the biblical narrative from that point onward will have been wondering who this serpent crusher will be. From Genesis 12:1-3 onward we know it will be one of the seed of Abraham. A child of Abraham will be a blessing for the redemption of the children of Adam.

> For just as through the disobedience of the one man the many were made sinners, so also through the obedience of the one man the many will be made righteous. (Rom 5:19)

Now of course when Paul wrote that, he was thinking of Jesus Christ. But it could have been said with relative theological validity about Abraham, for we are told that the obedience of Abraham was a key element in the confirmation of God's covenant with him for the blessing of all nations (Gen 22:16-18). And indeed it *was* said about Abraham in Jewish tradition long before Paul. Abraham, some Jewish rabbis said, was God's "second Adam"—the one through whom God made a fresh start for humanity. Through Abraham, Old Testament Israel could be seen as the core of a new, redeemed human race.[5] Paul built on this understanding of the relationship between Abraham and Adam, and affirms that *Jesus,* the true seed of Abaham, is the one through whom that promise has become a reality. Jesus is the Savior through whom the blessing promised to Abraham becomes available to people from all nations (Gal 3).

Matthew begins his Gospel affirming that Jesus ("Yahweh is salvation") the Messiah was the son of Abraham. And he ends his Gospel with Jesus declaring the great mission mandate that would encompass all nations—just as God had promised Abraham. Jesus thus sets the church also under the authority of the Abrahamic mission. The words of Jesus to his disciples in Matthew 28:18-20, the so-called Great Commission, could be seen as a christological development and renewal of the original

Abrahamic commission. Just as God had said to Abraham, so now Christ tells his disciples, effectively, "Go . . . and be a blessing . . . and all nations on earth will be blessed through you."

Historical. Since the mission to "be a blessing" is given to Abraham *and his seed after him,* it necessarily takes on a *historical* dimension. Blessing in and of itself need not be a historical thing. Up to this point in Genesis, blessing has been simply a relatively static, inbuilt feature of the created order, the enjoyment of fruitfulness and abundance. However, by making blessing a *promise* for the future ("I will bless you") and a *command* to be carried on into the future ("be a blessing"), our text transforms blessing into a historical dynamic. Genesis 12:1-3 injects blessing into history. God here launches a mission that holds hope for the future. History will be the outworking of God's promise and command of blessing (just as history will also, of course, be the outworking of human sin and God's curse).

This double dimension of history is important (and it lies behind Jesus' parable of the wheat and the tares, for example). The unfolding biblical story of all the generations yet to come will give plenty more evidence of *human fallenness.* All the marks of the earliest stories in the Bible will replay themselves again and again. We will see constant repetitions of the disobedience of Adam and Eve, the jealousy and violence of Cain, the vengeance of Lamech, the corruption and violence of the generation of Noah, and the arrogant insecurity of Babel. Yes, history will be as fallen as we are.

But what we must look for as well, in the light of Genesis 12:1-3, are the footprints of *divine blessing* on the road of history—blessing received from God and blessing passed on to others. And this history of blessing is nothing less than the history of salvation. Genesis 12:1-3, then, launches redemptive history within the continuum of wider human history—all of which is also, of course, under the sovereign plan of God. And it launches that history as the history of mission—the mission that God takes upon himself in his categorical commitments to Abraham and

his offspring, and the mission that God lays upon Abraham in consequence—"be a blessing."

So then, we cannot separate our doctrine of salvation from our understanding of biblical history, for that is the sphere in which God has acted
to bring us the blessings of salvation. Salvation is not just a doctrine we
believe in, or a condition we find ourselves in. *Salvation is a story we participate in*—the story of what God initiated through Abraham and accomplished through Christ.

BLESSING IS COVENANTAL AND ETHICAL

Covenantal. As the Old Testament story proceeds, the nature of the
blessing that Israel enjoyed within the covenant becomes increasingly
specific. The people of Israel came to learn more and more of the blessings of God's salvation in their historical experience. This includes the
following at least (it would be a helpful exercise to spend some time putting Bible references beside each item on the list):

- God's compassionate awareness of their plight in Egypt—as God
  heard, saw and was concerned for their suffering

- God's faithfulness to his covenant promise to Abraham as a major motivation of the exodus

- God's provision of a deliverer and mediator, in the person of Moses

- God's mighty power exercised in justice against their Egyptian oppressors and in deliverance of the Hebrews from slavery there

- God's protective care and provision for their physical needs in the wilderness

- God's revelation of himself, his name, his character, his covenant and
  his law, at Sinai

- God's combination of specific acts of punishment on their constant
  rebellions, with an ongoing gracious forgiveness that refused to aban-
  don them or the covenant with them

- God's provision of the tabernacle as the place of his presence, along with the priesthood and sacrificial system as the means of dealing with the ever-present realities of sin and failure
- God's gift of land as the tangible symbol of their relationship with him, as their "inheritance," as the place of blessing and security
- God's raising up judges to deliver them in times of oppression
- God's choice of David as king, and the promise made to him about the "son of David" who would rule over God's people forever
- God's willingness to place his name in Jerusalem and his presence in the temple there, symbolizing his holy presence in the midst of his people

Now of course all the dimensions of blessing listed above as part of Old Testament Israel's historical experience were fully real. They were not just pictures. God really delivered real people from real oppression and gave them real freedom. And the Bible describes that real historical event as "salvation" and speaks of God as Savior precisely because he did these things.

Nevertheless, it is equally clear that even in the Old Testament the external events in themselves did not exhaust all that was meant by salvation. God saved the Israelites out of Egypt in order to bring them into relationship with himself—a relationship of trust, love, worship and obedience. Sadly, many of those who experienced the saving power of God in the events of the exodus did not in fact respond in that way and perished. That is how Paul describes the tragic sequence of events between the exodus and the wilderness wandering.

> For I do not want you to be ignorant of the fact, brothers, that our fore-fathers were all under the cloud and that they all passed through the sea. They were all baptized into Moses in the cloud and in the sea. They all ate the same spiritual food and drank the same spiritual drink; for they drank from the spiritual rock that accompanied them, and that rock was Christ. Nevertheless, God was not pleased with most of them; their bodies were scattered over the desert.

Now these things occurred as examples to keep us from setting our hearts on evil things as they did. Do not be idolaters, as some of them were; as it is written: "The people sat down to eat and drink and got up to indulge in pagan revelry." We should not commit sexual immorality, as some of them did—and in one day twenty-three thousand of them died. We should not test the Lord, as some of them did—and were killed by snakes. And do not grumble, as some of them did—and were killed by the destroying angel.

These things happened to them as examples and were written down as warnings for us, on whom the fulfillment of the ages has come. So, if you think you are standing firm, be careful that you don't fall! No temptation has seized you except what is common to man. And God is faithful; he will not let you be tempted beyond what you can bear. But when you are tempted, he will also provide a way out so that you can stand up under it. (1 Cor 10:1-13)

So the New Testament shows how the story of salvation in the Old Testament ultimately points beyond itself, to the fullness of salvation accomplished by Christ on the cross. It is not that a merely national or physical salvation is simply replaced by a spiritual salvation. Rather, the totality of God's saving power is revealed in both testaments. Only in Christ, however, can we possess that totality. That is why Paul can speak of Christ's presence even in the Old Testament events. All that constitutes God's work of salvation throughout the whole of history is "in Christ"—whether it is experienced by those who lived chronologically before the earthly lifetime of Jesus (as in the case of the Old Testament Israelites) or after it (as is the case for us).

Ethical. In all the events and actions listed above, Israel was called upon to respond in the same way as the paradigm that Abraham had set—that is, in faith and obedience. Blessing within the covenant thus includes knowledge of who the only true and living God is (through the revelation of his name, YHWH), and commitment to love and obey him in such a way that the blessing may continue to be enjoyed (Deut

4:32-40). *The blessing of covenantal salvation required the response of covenantal ethics.*

This is the theological framework in which we need to understand the law of the Old Testament. It was given to the Israelites *after* God had saved them, on his own initiative and out of his own grace and love. It was only after he had brought them out of Egypt that he called them to keep his covenant and obey his law. God acted first. Israel's obedience was to be a *response* to their salvation—not the means of *achieving* it, still less of *deserving* it. This is the clear point of the first words God spoke to Israel after he got them to Sinai, in Exodus 19.

> Then Moses went up to God, and the LORD called to him from the mountain and said, "This is what you are to say to the house of Jacob and what you are to tell the people of Israel: 'You yourselves have seen what I did to Egypt, and how I carried you on eagles' wings and brought you to myself. Now if you obey me fully and keep my covenant, then out of all nations you will be my treasured possession. Although the whole earth is mine, you will be for me a kingdom of priests and a holy nation.' These are the words you are to speak to the Israelites." (Ex 19:3-6)

The whole book of Deuteronomy climaxes in the powerful appeal to Israel to "choose life," i.e., to sustain the blessing in which they stood through the covenant promises of God, by living in loving, trusting and obedient relationship with their God (Deut 30). This did not mean, of course, that Israel ever did or ever could *deserve* the blessing of God or any of his great saving acts. It is a fundamental mistake to think that in the Old Testament blessing or salvation came as something *earned* through obedience. On the contrary, blessing is *intrinsic* to the covenant relationship established by God's saving grace. Obedience is the means of living within the sphere of blessing and enjoying it—never the means of earning or deserving it. Or to put it in another way: blessing is the fruit of being saved by God, and obedience is the means by which those who have experienced God's salvation continue to enjoying that fruit. Israel had already been saved by God (in the exodus), so their obedience could never earn that. However, their obedience was necessary in order to go on enjoying the benefit of their salvation. Otherwise, through disobedience they would find themselves thrown out of the land, out of the place of God's blessing.

This ethical dimension of blessing within the covenant relationship is another feature that protects biblical blessing from degenerating into the parody that is paraded in prosperity theology. Blessing is not just an automatic reflex, routinely doled out in response to certain prescribed inputs—prayers or faith. Blessing is not like a great heavenly cashbox of miracles stored up for you and just waiting to be claimed.

In Nigeria recently, where I was helping to facilitate a Preaching Seminar for Langham Partnership and the Nigeria Initiative for Expository Preaching, I spent a lot of time being driven to and from the conference venue in various cars. Almost always there was Christian music being played on the car stereo or radio. The theme was repeatedly one of miracles and blessings—all there just for the asking. "Just Take It," one song repeated again and again, and it was talking about "your miracle." Here and there in the song I heard reference to Abraham, blessings, miracles and all the riches awaiting me, if I would "just take it." "I'm gonna take it," sang the singer again and again. It seemed a long way from the repeated teaching of Jesus about self-denial and self-giving and servanthood. And it is certainly a perversion of the promise of God through Abraham.

The link between the blessing of God and the experience of material abundance is neither automatic nor mechanical. It is possible that God's blessing will include material abundance, and the Bible gives examples of people who experienced it in that way. But it is not necessarily so, and even in the Bible it certainly is not always so. Moses was more intimate with God than any other character in the Old Testament and undoubtedly experienced the blessings of that relationship, but we are never told that he was materially rich, or wanted to be. Prophets and psalmists all experienced God's blessing, yet some of them, like Jeremiah, clearly suffered greatly.

Also, we cannot make the link between blessing and wealth operate with a kind of *reverse* logic. That is, although God's blessing may indeed result in a person becoming wealthy, we cannot say that just because someone is wealthy, he or she must be under God's blessing. Nor can we say that because someone is poor or sick, he or she is under God's curse or judgment. The Bible shows clearly that sometimes material loss or physical suffering is definitely *not* to be explained as the result of disobedience (as the books of Job and Jeremiah illustrate). And conversely the Bible equally shows that sometimes people may be very wealthy, not at all as a result of God's blessing, but rather through wickedness and oppression (as Amos and other prophets made clear). The realities of injustice and oppression reduce some people to poverty (even though they are relatively innocent) and make other people very rich (even though they are manifestly wicked). This fact negates any simplistic direct correspondence between wealth (or the lack of it) and God's blessing (or the absence of it).

Returning to our main point—the covenantal nature of blessing—God called the Israelites to exercise faith, obedience and ethical loyalty to the demands of the covenant in bad times as well as good times—whether things went well or not. This is the powerful message of Deuteronomy 8. They could certainly expect and pray that if they lived in such obedience, then God would enable them to live within the sphere of his blessing and all it entailed in their everyday lives. But they should remember also that "man does not live by bread alone," and there were healthy lessons to be learned even in times of need and affliction.

BLESSING IS MULTINATIONAL AND CHRISTOLOGICAL

The bottom line of God's promise to Abraham was that all nations on earth would find blessing through him. This is a promise of such vast extent that it takes in the whole of geography and history and sets up the rest of the biblical story as the outworking of this great mission of God. Ultimately, of course, the New Testament shows that the promise could only be fulfilled through the saving work of the Lord Jesus Christ, and then through the ongoing mission of his followers to take the good news of that salvation to all nations on earth. The work of Christ and the mission of the church both constitute God keeping his promise to Abraham, his missional promise to bless all nations.

Multinational. God's promise that all nations would be blessed through Abraham and his descendants is so central that it is affirmed five times in Genesis, to Abraham, Isaac and Jacob, in the following texts (using my own literal translation):

- Genesis 12:3: Through you will be blessed all kinship groups of the earth.

- Genesis 18:18: Through him will be blessed all nations of the earth.

- Genesis 22:18: Through your seed all nations of the earth will bless themselves.

- Genesis 26:4-5: Through your seed all nations of the earth will bless themselves.

- Genesis 28:14: Through you will be blessed all kinship groups of the earth, and in your seed.

The key verb in Hebrew is, of course, *bārak,* "to bless." As my translation above shows, sometimes it is used in a form that is mainly passive ("will be blessed") and sometimes in a different form that is reflexive ("will bless themselves"). The passive implies that they will be blessed by God. The reflexive implies that people would use the name of Abraham in blessing one another. That is, either they will pray for themselves to be blessed as Abraham was, or they will pray a blessing for others using the name of Abraham (saying something like: "may God bless you like Abraham"; compare Gen 48:20; Ruth 4:11-12; Ps 72:17).

In effect, it does not really make much difference since the reflexive sense will entail being blessed by God anyway. For if someone uses the name of Abraham as a blessing—that is to say, they pray to be blessed as Abraham was—it presupposes that *they know about the God who blessed Abraham.* They know that Abraham is proof of this God's power to bless. Such people thereby acknowledge *both* Abraham *and* Abraham's God. But God had just said that he will bless those who "bless Abraham." So those who bless themselves by Abraham will end up being blessed by God, for he promises to do so. The reflexive sense implies the passive sense as an outcome.

But this leads one to see another good reason why the more reflexive sense is actually significant—more so than if a simple passive only had been used.

The reflexive form of the verb is *self-involving.* The act of blessing oneself by (the name of) Abraham, or counting oneself blessed through him, indicates (as I have just said) that one knows the *source* of the blessing. If somebody knows that Abraham is a model of blessing and then seeks to be blessed as Abraham was, then he or she must surely also know about *the God of Abraham* and be deliberately and explicitly seeking blessing from *that* God and not from *other* gods.

Now, actually, a person may "be blessed" (in a purely passive sense) without necessarily knowing or acknowledging the source of the blessing. Tragically, many people (including many within Old Testament Israel) attribute to other gods (or to their own achievements) the blessings they have received from the living creator God. They get the blessings but give the credit to false gods or to themselves. So the fact is that people can passively enjoy "being blessed" by God (with life, health, food, friends, the good gifts of creation) *without ever coming to know God* or to love and worship him. As Paul saw clearly in Romans 1, people may take all the blessings of God but deliberately refuse to know him and suppress the truth about him.

But a person cannot intentionally and specifically invoke *blessing in the name of Abraham* without acknowledging the source of Abraham's blessing, namely, Abraham's God. So the reflexive form of the verb indicates some form of self-involvement with the God of Abraham, some willingness to acknowledge that Abraham's blessing is the kind of blessing that I want too, and from the same God who blessed Abraham.

There is thus what we might call a confessional dimension to the anticipated blessing of the nations. People from all nations will be blessed as they come to acknowledge the God of Abraham and "bless themselves" in and through him. The extension of the blessing of salvation to the nations will be an exercise in the extension of the *knowledge of God* among the nations.

Clearly, then, God's intention at this climax of his promise to Abraham is not merely that all nations should be blessed (purely passive) in some vague and general way, regardless of their relationship with Abraham, or independent of what God has promised to do for Abraham. No, the combined force of the crucial word *"through you"* with the self-involving reflexive form of the verb shows that God's intention is that nations will self-consciously share in the blessing of Abraham through deliberate appropriation of it for themselves. This is not just randomly sprinkled blessing. The nations will indeed come to be blessed as Abraham was, but only because they will have turned to the only source of such blessing, Abraham's God, and identified themselves with the story of Abraham's people. They will know the God of Abraham. That is where blessing and salvation are to be found.

As God's promise to Abraham unfolds in the vision of the Old Testament Scriptures, it takes on many forms. The theme of "the nations" is actually much more prominent in the Old Testament than is acknowledged in many textbooks on Old Testament theology. It is particularly exciting to see what the Old Testament says about the future of the nations in relation to God's plan of salvation. Of course there would be judgment (as there would also be on Israel). But through and beyond judgment, many psalms and many passages in the prophets envisage people from all nations coming to share in the saving blessing that God promised through Abraham.[6] Just scan through this brief survey of the way the Old Testament describes the coming blessing and salvation of people from all the nations. Do take time at this point to read the texts in brackets and reflect on their implications as regards God's great missional intention for the blessing and salvation of the nations:

- They will come to benefit from, and to praise God for, all the blessings enjoyed by Israel (Ps 47; 67).

- They will come to worship Israel's God (Ps 2:10-11; 22:27-28; 68:31-32; 86:8-10; 96:1-3; 117:1-2; 102:15, 21-22; 138:4-5; 145:10-12; 148:11; Is 2:1-5; 12:4-5; 18:7; 23:17-18; 24:14-16; 42:10-12; 45:6, 14; 60; 61:5-7; 66:18-19).

- They will be registered in God's city—Zion (Ps 87).

- They will be blessed with God's salvation (Is 19:16-25).

- They will be accepted in God's house (Is 56:3-8).

- They will be called by God's name (Amos 9:11-12).

- They will be joined with God's people—Israel (Zech 2:10-12; 9:7).

So the fulfillment of God's promise to Abraham comes about not merely as nations are blessed in some general or anonymous sense, but only as they specifically come to know the whole biblical grand story of salvation, of which Abraham is a key starting point and Abraham's God is the key player. And in coming to know this story, and in turning in repentance and faith toward this God, other nations actually become part of God's people—the people of the Israel of God who were a single nation in the Old Testament but are now constituted by people from all nations who turn to God through Christ. According to these many Old Testament texts, the nations will have the opportunity to experience God's salvation through becoming part of God's redeemed people, sharing and benefiting from their story. So the story of Old Testament Israel becomes the story and the inheritance of people of all nations who come to faith in the living God. This story is our story—whoever and wherever we are, of whatever ethnic background—once we become part of this people through faith in Christ.

Christological. This is profoundly important for mission. One of the reasons for the appalling shallowness and vulnerability of much that passes for the growth of the church around the world is that people are coming to some kind of instrumental faith in a God they see as powerful. They discern that Jesus is the name through which this power of God is released, and they look for all the blessings that they can have in the name of Jesus, but with very little knowledge of who Jesus was or is, in the context of any biblical understanding.

Or, to the contrary, some people may choose *not* to exercise faith in Jesus because they are under the impression that he is only there to meet needs or aspirations that are not relevant to them.

Another Nigerian friend told me about a businessman he met. For many years this man had felt no need to become a Christian. The reason was because of a poster he regularly passed in his car on his way to work. It was presumably intended as an evangelistic message, but it had precisely the opposite effect. "Are you or your family sick?" it asked, with the answer, "You need Jesus." "Are you struggling to make ends meet? You need Jesus. Is your business failing? You need Jesus. Are you lonely? You need Jesus." And so it went on with a list of reasons why the reader should turn to Jesus.

But this businessman suffered from none of the listed problems. So, as he told my friend, "I didn't fit into any of the categories that would have made me want to be a Christian." None of the categories, incidentally, included any moral need or failing. There was no mention of *sin,* no suggestion that Jesus is the one through whom we have forgiveness of sin. So this person had no felt needs for which the Jesus on offer on the poster had anything to give him. Why should he want to be a Christian if all Jesus could offer was answers to needs he didn't have?

What a travesty of the gospel! Yet it is sadly all too common, if not quite so crass, in many popular evangelistic messages. So when vulnerable people who do have genuine needs are offered this Jesus-will-meet-your-needs package, they jump to say they "have faith" in this Jesus, and then wait expectantly for the preacher's promises to be delivered.

Now, I'm sure this is often a very sincere and simple faith, according to what they have been told through Christian evangelism or personal witness. But so often their faith seems to be directed toward a Jesus disconnected from his scriptural roots. They have been told nothing about the great biblical story of which Jesus is the completion and fulfillment. As a result of this ignorance, they have not been challenged at the level of their deeper worldview by coming to know God *in and through the story that is launched by Abraham.* For it is in that great story in the Old Testament that we learn so much, not only about who the living God is, but also about what he expects from his people within the covenant relationship—especially in terms of his ethical demands of love, justice, compassion and integrity. There is, in other words, no real challenge at the level of inner core beliefs and the radical demands of discipleship and transformed, Christlike living.

Jesus came as the incarnation of the God of Abraham, as the one who fulfilled the mission of God through Old Testament Israel, as the Lord who called for the same quality of life and behavior in his disciples. We need to know Jesus in all his biblical depth and background if we are fully to understand the nature of the salvation and blessing that he brings.

Now Paul had not left his converts vulnerable at this level. Paul planted churches among Gentiles—foreigners (as far as the Jews were concerned), people who had no background knowledge at all of the Old Testament. Yet it is clear that Paul had taught them very thoroughly that by coming to faith in Jesus they had also come to belong to the people of God, the covenant people of Abraham. Read Galatians 3 and Ephesians 2–3. They too had a share in the story and the promises of Old Testament Israel. In fact, they had come to belong *within* biblical Israel as God's people. Or more precisely, God's people Israel had been *expanded* (through Christ and in the purpose of God) to include people of foreign nations who, so long as they are in Christ, are now to be counted as also in Abraham. Why? Because Jesus is *the Christ*—the Messiah, who embodied Old Testament Israel in his own person. So all those in him are by that very fact included in the Israel of God in Christ.

And what Paul told the Christians of Galatia and Ephesus, of course, applies to Christian believers of any nation, including yours and mine— anywhere in the world.

All those who are *in Christ* are thereby also embedded in the faith and spiritual lineage of *Abraham.* These Gentile believers had turned to the living God from their dead idols (1 Thess 1:9). But the living God they had turned to was none other than the God of Abraham. And this God had even announced the gospel in advance to Abraham, saying that all nations would be blessed through him (Gal 3:8). In other words, it had always been (and still is) God's intention that the people of Abraham would not be confined to his ethnic descendants, or to Old Testament Israelites, but would expand to include people from any and every nation. So now these new Christians, who were not ethnically Jews at all, were included in the people of Abraham and could count themselves blessed in him, through his Seed, the Messiah Jesus. For, "those who have faith [i.e., in Jesus Christ] are blessed along with Abraham, the man of faith" (Gal 3:9).

> For all of you [Gentiles] are children of God through faith in Christ [Messiah] Jesus, for as many of you who were baptized into Christ have clothed yourselves with Christ. There is no longer Jew or Greek, no longer slave or free, no longer male or female, for all of you are one in Christ Jesus. If you belong to Christ, then you are Abraham's descendants [seed], his heirs according to the promise. (Gal 3:26-29, my translation)

And following Paul, of course, we who read Genesis 12:1-3 as Christian believers know that its fulfillment is rooted in that same Jesus. The multinational vision of the great promise of God to Abraham is possible only through Christ. That is why the Christian faith has been a missionary faith from the beginning. The gospel has to be proclaimed to all nations because the promise of God means blessing for all nations and that Christ died for people from all nations. That is the full christological significance of the blessing of Abraham, as a result of which the good news of salvation can be preached to the ends of the earth.

Calvin recognized that the full dimensions of Genesis 12:1-3 can only be grasped by setting it in the context of the work of Christ. Indeed, he observes, since Christ was "in the loins of Abraham" (i.e., Jesus would be the son of Abraham in his human descent), the promise was already christological in origin.

> We must understand that the blessing was promised to Abram in Christ, when he was coming into the land of Canaan. Therefore, God (in my judgment) pronounces that all nations should be blessed in his servant Abram because Christ was included in his body. In this manner, he not only intimates that Abram would be an *example,* but a *cause* of blessing. . . . [Paul] concludes that the covenant of salvation that God made with Abram is neither stable nor firm except in Christ. I therefore thus interpret the present place as saying that God promises to his servant Abram that blessing that will afterwards flow to all people.[7]

It is of the essence of the biblical gospel, first announced to Abraham, that God has indeed made such blessing for all nations—the blessing of salvation—available through the Messiah, Jesus of Nazareth, the seed of Abraham. In Christ alone, through the gospel of his death and resurrection, stands the hope of blessing for all nations.

QUESTIONS FOR REFLECTION OR DISCUSSION

1. How would you explain to someone "the blessings of salvation" in a way that included the full biblical meaning of blessing and yet avoided the false teaching of the "prosperity gospel"?

2. In what ways is your understanding of the Old Testament changed or improved by recognizing the importance of God's promise to Abra-

ham as God's answer to the sin of Adam, and connecting both to the obedience and death of Christ?

3. "Salvation does not mean rescuing people *out of* creation to some other realm, but bringing back God's blessing *into* creation, through God's redeeming and transforming power. Salvation, then, is God's mission of redemptive blessing, restoring his whole creation to what was lost because of human sin and rebellion." What difference should it make to your concept of mission and practice of evangelism that salvation in the Bible is ultimately for the whole creation, not just for individual souls?

4

Salvation and God's Covenant Story

"SALVATION BELONGS TO *OUR GOD*." WE CONTINUE to think about the rich content of the last two words of this phrase. It is, as I said in the last chapter, a strongly covenantal way of speaking, with deep roots in the Old Testament. To speak of "our God" is to speak of the God who engaged with the biblical people of Israel throughout their long historical journey in the Old Testament—and of course on into its climax in the New Testament.

Indeed, the story of the covenants in the Bible is the story of God, and vice versa. God engaged with real people in real history, and the Bible is the story of that engagement. It is also the story of salvation, for all God's covenants have a single unifying thread—salvation. The succession of covenants recorded in the Bible is like a series of signposts in the developing story of God's saving response to the plight of humanity. Each one points forward to the next, and all of them together point forward to God's ultimate saving purpose for creation and humanity. In fact, to trace the sequence of major covenants within the Bible is a very useful way of seeing the Bible as a whole, that is, to see the coherent plot that runs through it all. So let us survey them very briefly in order.[1]

The Covenant Sequence

Noah.

The LORD smelled the pleasing aroma and said in his heart: "Never again will I curse the ground because of man, even though every inclination of his heart is evil from childhood. And never again will I destroy all living creatures, as I have done.

> "As long as the earth endures,
> seedtime and harvest,
> cold and heat,
> summer and winter,
> day and night
> will never cease." (Gen 8:21-22)

Then God said to Noah and to his sons with him: "I now establish my covenant with you and with your descendants after you and with every living creature that was with you—the birds, the livestock and all the wild animals, all those that came out of the ark with you—every living creature on earth. I establish my covenant with you: Never again will all life be cut off by the waters of a flood; never again will there be a flood to destroy the earth."

And God said, "This is the sign of the covenant I am making between me and you and every living creature with you, a covenant for all generations to come: I have set my rainbow in the clouds, and it will be the sign of the covenant between me and the earth. Whenever I bring clouds over the earth and the rainbow appears in the clouds, I will remember my covenant between me and you and all living creatures of every kind. Never again will the waters become a flood to destroy all life. Whenever the rainbow appears in the clouds, I will see it and remember the everlasting covenant between God and all living creatures of every kind on the earth."

So God said to Noah, "This is the sign of the covenant I have established between me and all life on the earth." (Gen 9:8-17)

The covenant with Noah, recorded in Genesis 8:20–9:17, ensures the continuation of life on earth—it provides the universal platform on which it has been possible for us to live as a sinful human race on a cursed planet with some assurance of survival. It is the broadest of all the covenants since in it God makes a promise in relation to the earth as a whole—not just to human beings. It was made after the flood—a story that simultaneously included God's judgment on the sinful world and God's salvation of Noah and his family.

So the covenant with Noah rests, like the other covenants, on God's saving grace and God's strong will to bless. It points toward an ultimately good future for the earth and humanity.

Abraham. The covenant with Abraham, as we saw in chapter three, is the starting point of salvation history in the Bible. It launches the community of blessing, those who will both be blessed in their relationship with God and be the means of all nations coming into the experience of God's blessing. It is first recorded in Genesis 12:1-3, but fresh and expanding articulations of it are also presented in Genesis 15, 17 and 22.

The covenant with Abraham links our understanding of salvation both to our ecclesiology and to our missiology.

That is to say, on the one hand, Abraham is the father of the community of God's people—the physical ancestor of the Israelites in the Old Testament, and the spiritual ancestor of those from every nation who will be saved through Christ. As Paul wrote, explaining the essential unity of all those who share the faith of Abraham,

> Therefore, the promise comes by faith, so that it may be by grace and may be guaranteed to all Abraham's offspring—not only to those who are of the law but also to those who are of the faith of Abraham. He is the father of us all. As it is written: "I have made you a father of many nations." He is our father in the sight of God, in whom he believed. (Rom 4:16-17)

And on the other hand, the covenant with Abraham included God's promise that through him and his people, blessing would extend to all nations. That is God's mission, and thereby also the mission of God's people. Those who enjoy the blessing of Abraham (which means all of us who are in Christ—hence the ecclesiological point just emphasized above) are those who are commissioned to be the agents of bringing that blessing to others (hence the missiological point also).

Salvation, then, in the light of the Abrahamic covenant, cannot be individualistic:

- Biblical salvation is not something I enjoy all by myself; it makes me part of the community of God's people (ecclesiology).

- And biblical salvation is not something I can keep all to myself; it demands that I share its blessing with others (mission).

Moses. The covenant at Sinai through Moses bound the national community of Old Testament Israel to Yahweh in the wake of God's mighty act of salvation, the exodus. It is made abundantly clear that this saving action itself was based on the foundation of the covenant with Abraham. God acted to deliver Israel from Egypt because he "remembered" his promise to Abraham (Ex 2:24; 3:6, 15; 6:2-8). This does not mean that he had temporarily "forgotten" it. Rather, it means that the time had come for God to take action upon his promise.

So we should not think of the Sinai covenant as separate from, or superior to, the covenant with Abraham. Rather, Sinai was the consolidation of what God had promised to Abraham now that one part of that promise had been fulfilled—namely, his descendants had now become a great nation (Ex 1:7). God's mission (his ultimate purpose) remained the same—to bless the nations through these people descended from Abraham. But as a whole people, the Israelites too must respond to him as Abraham had done—in faith and obedience. That was the essence of the Sinai covenant relationship.

The preamble to the giving of the law and covenant at Sinai makes clear both its origin in the saving work of God himself ("I brought you up out of Egypt") and its purpose in relation to Israel's place in the midst of all the nations of the earth who also belong to God ("the whole earth is mine").

You yourselves have seen what I did to Egypt, and how I carried you on
eagles' wings and brought you to myself. Now if you obey me fully and
keep my covenant, then out of all nations you will be my treasured pos-
session. Although the whole earth is mine, you will be for me a kingdom
of priests and a holy nation. (Ex 19:4-6)

In order to give shape and substance to that covenantal obedience,
the Sinai covenant included God's law. But that too was a gift of grace,
intended to shape Israel into the holy and distinctive people that they
needed to be as God's "priesthood" in the midst of the nations. The covenant law comes *after* the exodus. That is, we have eighteen chapters of
salvation in Exodus before we have a single chapter of law. Only after the
story of salvation do we come to Sinai (Ex 19), the ten commandments
(Ex 20) and the making of the covenant (Ex 24).

The Sinai covenant, like all biblical covenants, is founded on God's
grace and motivated by God's *mission.* That is to say, it looks *back* to what
God had already done for Israel out of his love and grace in delivering
them from slavery, and it looks *forward* to God's purpose within history
through Israel—to make them the instrument of his blessing to the nations. The law is connected to both of these perspectives. So we should
not try to interpret the laws of the Old Testament in isolation from the
narrative and theological context in which they are set. They were not
given as a means for Israel to achieve or deserve God's salvation. Nor
were they given as timeless rules to be universally imposed with wooden
literalism. Rather, they were given to people whom God had already redeemed, to enable them, within their own cultural and historical context, to respond rightly to God's saving grace and to live in ways that
would show the character and will of God to the nations.

David. The establishment of kingship in Israel was flawed with human failure and wrong motives. But God, as so often, takes up even
flawed human initiatives and builds them into his own sovereign and
saving purpose. So God made his covenant with David (2 Sam 7).

Now then, tell my servant David, "This is what the LORD Almighty says: I took you from the pasture and from following the flock to be ruler over my people Israel. I have been with you wherever you have gone, and I have cut off all your enemies from before you. Now I will make your name great, like the names of the greatest men of the earth. And I will provide a place for my people Israel and will plant them so that they can have a home of their own and no longer be disturbed. Wicked people will not oppress them anymore, as they did at the beginning and have done ever since the time I appointed leaders over my people Israel. I will also give you rest from all your enemies.

"The LORD declares to you that the LORD himself will establish a house for you: When your days are over and you rest with your fathers, I will raise up your offspring to succeed you, who will come from your own body, and I will establish his kingdom. He is the one who will build a house for my Name, and I will establish the throne of his kingdom forever. I will be his father, and he will be my son. When he does wrong, I will punish him with the rod of men, with floggings inflicted by men. But my love will never be taken away from him, as I took it away from Saul, whom I removed from before you. Your house and your kingdom will endure forever before me; your throne will be established forever." (2 Sam 7:8-16)

Once again we notice that the initiative came from God, and was an act of his grace and love. David could only respond with surprise and gratitude.

The covenant with David in some ways echoes the covenant with Abraham:

- The Davidic covenant is made with an individual, but with implications for those who would be his descendants.

- God promises to make David's name great.

- God also promises him a son, through whom the promise will continue.

Beyond that, the covenant with David eventually became the foundation of the *messianic hope* in the Old Testament—that is, the expectation that God would raise up a true Son of David, who would save God's people from all their enemies, and then rule over the people of God, in perfect peace and justice, and forever. The New Testament, of course, sees the fulfillment of the Davidic covenant ultimately in Jesus.

New Covenant. The long line of kings in Judah and Israel went from bad to worse (with a few notable exceptions, like Hezekiah and Josiah). The people fell into ever deeper pits of rebellion against God and neglect of his law and covenant. In the end, God declared that the threats inherent in the covenant must be fulfilled, and so in punishment God sent Israel into exile. Jerusalem was destroyed by Nebuchadnezzar, and the people were taken off into captivity in Babylon.

But the promise to Abraham was never forgotten. Beyond judgment, there was still hope because of the faithfulness of God to his own declared mission. This was what many of the pre-exilic prophets had said, and it was reaffirmed by prophets at the time of the exile.

And so there arose the vision of a new covenant. This was not conceived as something radically different in kind from the original covenant. Rather, it promised a more complete and perfect enjoyment of the relationship between God and his people. The clearest articulation is found in Jeremiah 31:31-34, which is all the more familiar to us because it is quoted twice in the epistle to the Hebrews. It is Jeremiah who articulates this with the exact words "a new covenant."

> "The time is coming," declares the LORD,
>   "when I will make a new covenant
> with the house of Israel
>   and with the house of Judah.
> It will not be like the covenant
>   I made with their forefathers
> when I took them by the hand
>   to lead them out of Egypt,
> because they broke my covenant,

though I was a husband to them,"
   declares the LORD.
"This is the covenant I will make with the house of Israel
   after that time," declares the LORD.
"I will put my law in their minds
   and write it on their hearts.
I will be their God,
   and they will be my people.
No longer will a man teach his neighbor,
   or a man his brother, saying, 'Know the LORD,'
because they will all know me,
   from the least of them to the greatest,"
   declares the LORD.
"For I will forgive their wickedness
   and will remember their sins no more." (Jer 31:31-34)

But the concept and the promise of a new covenant arrangement between God and his people are found in several other places in the prophets.

Ezekiel, in chapters 34—37, envisages the future restoration and re-establishment of Israel itself in language that has echoes of all the covenants with Noah, with David and at Sinai (e.g., Ezek 34:23-31). The whole flavour of Ezekiel's vision of the future is strongly covenantal.

The book of Isaiah uses the language of covenant to express future hope in universalizing ways that include the nations. In Isaiah 42:6 and Isaiah 49:6, the mission of the servant of the LORD is, among other things, to be a "covenant for the people"—which is surely to be understood through its parallelism with "light for the nations." The Davidic covenant is referred to in Isaiah 55:3-5, but in a way that universalizes it and extends it to the nations. Even the covenant with Noah is harnessed to the certainty of God's promise of future blessing for his people, in Isaiah 54:7-10.

All this Old Testament prophecy about a new covenant is taken up in the New Testament, of course, and applied to Jesus. He is seen as the one who brings about the new covenant, and thus sets in motion its great extension to all the nations—in fulfillment of the covenant promise to Abraham. Jesus himself, in his last supper, the Passover meal he ate before his crucifixion, spoke of the wine in these massively significant terms: "This cup is the new covenant in my blood, which is poured out for you" (Lk 22:20). In other words, the blood of Jesus, shed on the cross, sealed the new covenant, through which salvation and forgiveness are made possible.

Not surprisingly, then, the documents which eventually were brought together to witness to Jesus, to tell the story of his death and resurrection, the gift of the Spirit, and the early mission of his followers to the Gentile nations, are collectively entitled "the New Covenant" (for that is what *testament* means). The unity of the Old Testament and the New Testament is fundamentally covenantal.

Finally, the Bible shows us the perfect completion of God's covenant with Abraham in the book of Revelation. In fact, all the great Bible covenants are there in the book of Revelation.

- *Noah* is there in the vision of a new creation, a new heaven and a new earth after judgment.

- *Abraham* is there in the ingathering and blessing of all nations from every tongue and language.

- *Moses* is there in the covenantal assertion that "they will be his people, and God himself will be with them and be their God," and "the dwelling of God is with men, and he will live with them" (Rev 21:3).

- *David* is there in the Holy City, the new Jerusalem, and in the identity of Jesus as the Lion of Judah and Root of David.

- *The New Covenant* is there in the fact that all of this will be accomplished by the blood of the Lamb who was slain.

This is the grand climax of the long sweep of covenantal history through the whole Bible. All the covenants together proclaim the mission of God as his committed promise to the nations and to the whole of creation. The book of Revelation could be regarded as the final covenantal declaration: "Mission accomplished."

Salvation—the story. Now that we have surveyed the great sweep of biblical covenants, what have we learned? We see yet again the importance of salvation history—which was mentioned also in the last chapter. The point is that salvation in the Bible, because it is embodied in these historical covenants, is not merely a set of doctrines to be learned. Salvation is not just a subjective personal experience to be enjoyed by myself. Salvation is not some mythical future state of paradise that I long to arrive at by whatever religious methods I think will achieve it.

Salvation is fundamentally a story—The Story. Salvation is constituted within the all-encompassing biblical metanarrative that forms the biblical worldview.

The Bible is fundamentally a grand narrative with four major parts or sections:

creation—fall—redemption in history—new creation

And salvation, as biblically defined, is all that is contained in the third and fourth parts of that great story: redemption in history and the future hope of new creation. Salvation spans the great arch of history from God's covenant with Abraham to the second coming of Christ. The story of salvation is what fills the gap between the scattering of the nations in Genesis 11 and the healing of the nations in Revelation 22. The Bible is, above all else, the story of salvation.

All the particular historical moments within the story of salvation, and all the theories and definitions that we choose to make when we try to explain our doctrine of salvation, only make sense within that overarching narrative framework. The gospel is not somebody's theory. It is not somebody's *good idea.* The gospel is the *good news* about what the biblical God has done, is doing and will finally do, within the history of the world. That is why it is so important, as I have repeatedly emphasized, that we use our whole Bible in coming to an understanding of salvation, and not rely solely on a few isolated verses of doctrinal teaching from Paul's letters.

For even Paul, when he talks about salvation, typically has the whole story of Old Testament biblical Israel in mind—along with its fulfillment in Christ. Paul lived in that biblical-narrative world. When he thought of salvation, he thought of the Old Testament story. His understanding of God's salvation was rooted in that world. So, along with the Scriptures, Paul looked back to God's election and call of Abraham, and his redemption of Israel. And equally along with the Scriptures, Paul looked forward to God's promise for the future blessing of all nations, to be accomplished through the mission of the Messiah and the proclamation of the gospel.

One lovely example of how Paul's mind instinctively thought of salvation within this historical sequence is in 2 Thessalonians:

> But we ought always to thank God for you, brothers loved by the Lord, because from the beginning God chose you to be saved through the sanctifying work of the Spirit and through belief in the truth. He called you to this through our gospel, that you might share in the glory of our Lord Jesus Christ. (2 Thess 2:13-14)

Just look at the sequence of God's actions that Paul lists as being included in the Thessalonians' salvation. These Thessalonian believers (and all of us who are believers like them) have been

- loved by the Lord
- chosen by God
- saved by God
- sanctified by the Spirit
- called to faith in the truth of the gospel
- destined to share in Christ's glory

Now that is a sequence which, whether intentionally or not in the mind of Paul, reflects the story of Old Testament Israel: God loved them, chose them in Abraham, saved them from Egypt, constituted them as his holy (sanctified) people at Sinai, revealed his truth to them, called them to obedient faith and promised them a glorious future inheritance. Paul's whole conception of salvation has been shaped by that story, which of course he sees as now fulfilled and realized in the gospel of Christ. So much so that, even when Paul simply wants to list the great blessings of salvation that believers have received, he cannot help arranging them in the order of the Old Testament story of salvation. As I said, this may not be conscious or intentional on the part of Paul, but it is revealing of the way he instinctively frames his description of the work and content of salvation. What God has done for us in Christ is like a glorious recapitulation on an infinitely grander scale of what God had done for Old Testament Israel.

Salvation in both testaments is a story that stretches, as 2 Thessalonians 2:13-14 portrays, from the eternity of God's love to the eternity of Christ's glory. That is the vast, universal and eternal context within which my own and your own personal salvation is to be located, along with all those in the whole of human history who will share in this story through Christ, and sing of it in the new creation.

SALVATION: PAST, PRESENT AND FUTURE

Whether we look at salvation in the Old or in the New Testament, we find that it has this storied quality. And that in turn means that salvation can be described in terms of the past, the present and the future.

There are parts of the story that lie in the past—they have happened in history and nothing can change that. *We have been saved.* But God's people also live in a continuous present, and so they frequently appeal to God to act "now" to save us. *We are being saved.* And we know that the world is not yet transformed into the place God has promised it will be. We look forward to the completion and full enjoyment of our salvation. *We shall be saved.*

Imagine that you are at sea and your ship has had a disaster and is sinking. As the ship goes down, you jump into the sea, where you are in danger of drowning. But in that moment of mortal danger, a lifeboat comes past and someone pulls you out of the water into the boat. You have been saved from drowning in the sea. But you are not yet finally rescued. In the lifeboat you hear the good news that the captain was able to radio to the shore to summon the coastguard. The rescue helicopter is on its way. You will be saved when the helicopter arrives and lifts you all to safety and back to dry land. You have been saved, you are in a safe place now, and you will be saved. The biblical story of salvation has all three tenses also.

Once again, let us scan our Bibles for all three tenses of salvation in both testaments.

Salvation in the past tense. In the Old Testament, the Israelites looked back to the exodus as the great saving event of their history. They celebrated it and relived it in the annual Passover—as Jews still do (Ex 12). Once they settled in the land of promise, Israelite farmers were instructed to make a declaration every harvest which affirmed the "givenness" of their redemption out of slavery and the gift of the land. It is a remarkable affirmation, which has something of the character of a creed. It binds together several centuries of past history but also brings it right up to the present moment—as present as the harvest just gathered—and makes it entirely personal in its effects.

> When you have entered the land the LORD your God is giving you as an inheritance and have taken possession of it and settled in it, take some of the firstfruits of all that you produce from the soil of the land the LORD your God is giving you and put them in a basket. Then go to the place the LORD your God will choose as a dwelling for his Name and say to the priest in office at the time, "I declare today to the LORD your God that I have come to the land the LORD swore to our forefathers to give us." The priest shall take the basket from your hands and set it down in front of the altar of the LORD your God. Then you shall declare before the LORD

your God: "My father was a wandering Aramean, and he went down into Egypt with a few people and lived there and became a great nation, powerful and numerous. But the Egyptians mistreated us and made us suffer, putting us to hard labor. Then we cried out to the LORD, the God of our fathers, and the LORD heard our voice and saw our misery, toil and oppression. So the LORD brought us out of Egypt with a mighty hand and an outstretched arm, with great terror and with miraculous signs and wonders. He brought us to this place and gave us this land, a land flowing with milk and honey; and now I bring the firstfruits of the soil that you, O LORD, have given me." Place the basket before the LORD your God and bow down before him. And you and the Levites and the aliens among you shall rejoice in all the good things the LORD your God has given to you and your household. (Deut 26:1-11)

Israelite fathers were similarly instructed that when their children asked for an explanation about the law God had given to Israel, they were to tell the story—the old, old story of Yahweh and his love. The meaning of the law and motivation for obeying it were to be found in the fact and the story of salvation. Salvation was a fact of the past, with implications for obedience in the present.

In the future, when your son asks you, "What is the meaning of the stipulations, decrees and laws the LORD our God has commanded you?" tell him: "We were slaves of Pharaoh in Egypt, but the LORD brought us out of Egypt with a mighty hand. Before our eyes the LORD sent miraculous signs and wonders—great and terrible—upon Egypt and Pharaoh and his whole household. But he brought us out from there to bring us in and give us the land that he promised on oath to our forefathers. The LORD commanded us to obey all these decrees and to fear the LORD our God, so that we might always prosper and be kept alive, as is the case today. And if we are careful to obey all this law before the LORD our God, as he has commanded us, that will be our righteousness." (Deut 6:20-25)

Turning to the New Testament, Paul can speak of the God who *has saved us*, using the form of the Greek verb that normally speaks of something that has happened in the past but continues to have ongoing, present effects.

> For it is by grace *you have been saved,* through faith—and this not from yourselves, it is the gift of God—not by works, so that no one can boast. (Eph 2:8-9, my italics)

And he can also use the Greek verb form that often expresses something wholly in the past—whether he has in mind the completed work of Christ on the cross or the fact of our regeneration through the Holy Spirit. Our salvation, in these passages of Paul, is something that God has already accomplished, and so we look back to it as a given fact, with gratitude.

> We ourselves, who have the firstfruits of the Spirit, groan inwardly as we wait eagerly for our adoption as sons, the redemption of our bodies. For in this hope *we were saved.* (Rom 8:23-24, my italics)

> *He saved us,* not because of righteous things we had done, but because of his mercy. He saved us through the washing of rebirth and renewal by the Holy Spirit. (Tit 3:5, my italics; see also Col 1:13)

Salvation in the present tense. Old Testament Israel constantly cried out to God for help and salvation in the present tense of their struggles, individually and nationally. In fact, the narratives show that God's great historical acts of salvation in the past were motivated by the crying out of Israel at that "present" time.

> During that long period, the king of Egypt died. The Israelites groaned in their slavery and cried out, and their cry for help because of their slavery went up to God. God heard their groaning and he remembered his covenant with Abraham, with Isaac and with Jacob. So God looked on the Israelites and was concerned about them. (Ex 2:23-25)

No wonder then, that the great confidence of the psalmists was that "God is our refuge and strength, an *ever-present* help in trouble" (Ps 46:1, my italics).

Likewise, Isaiah delights to affirm that Yahweh is always contemporary. He has been there from before the beginning and will be there beyond the end—he is never out of date, never an anachronism, never ahead of his time. He is always the God of the present (Is 43:10; 44:6; 46:10). For that reason, God can be trusted to bring his salvation right into the present.

Turning again to the New Testament, Paul sometimes speaks of believers as those who "are being saved." Salvation is an ongoing process, something that goes on happening in the circumstances of life. So, for example, Paul distinguishes between those who "are perishing" and those who "are being saved": "For the message of the cross is foolishness to those who are perishing, but to *us who are being saved* it is the power of God" (1 Cor 1:18, my italics; see also 2 Cor 2:15).

Then also, Paul portrays salvation as a present process that has to be worked out in our lives in obedient fear of God.

> Therefore, my dear friends, as you have always obeyed—not only in my presence, but now much more in my absence—continue to *work out your salvation* with fear and trembling, for it is God who works in you to will and to act according to his good purpose. (Phil 2:12-13, my italics)

This does not mean that salvation is something we can *achieve* for ourselves, or that we have to make arrangements for our own salvation. It means we have to *live out* in practical daily experience the implications of the fact that we have experienced the salvation of God in Christ, as he works in us. Salvation is a present reality that affects our lives and our lifestyle. It is not just a past experience (in our "testimony") or a future longing (for heaven when we die). It is an existential condition of our present life on earth. We are to live as those who are experiencing God's salvation at work in our lives.

Peter means much the same when he urges his readers to "grow up in your salvation" (1 Pet 2:2). This does not mean that we can grow to be more saved than we already are. It means that humble discipleship and growing maturity are the fruit and evidence of salvation in our present lives.

In the same way, we might talk about a young couple growing up in their marriage. It does not mean that they become more married as time goes by, for that is a given status from the day of their wedding. Rather, it means that each one learns more and more how to live for the sake of the other and to strengthen the bonds and the blessings of their married relationship. So it is as we "grow up in salvation"—it is an ever-present challenge and privilege for the person who has been, and will be, saved.

Salvation in the future tense. In the Old Testament, as we saw in the last chapter, there is an increasing eschatological hope of the coming salvation that Yahweh would accomplish, not only for his people but also for the nations. Salvation was a great future prospect, based on their experience of salvation as a great historical fact in the past.

"The day of the LORD" seems originally to have been associated with such hopes. The Israelites believed that the day would come when God would save them by destroying their enemies and exalting them to top nation. Amos was the first to subvert this popular conception, and to warn Israel, in their state of covenant-breaking disobedience, idolatry and social evil, that the day of the LORD would bring terrible judgment upon them (Amos 5:18-24). As indeed it did, in the immediate context of the devastation of defeat and exile. Most prophets after Amos who spoke about the day of the LORD also made it devastatingly clear that it would bring judgment.

However, beyond judgment there always lay hope, with the God of Israel, as Deuteronomy 30 had assured them. And so Zephaniah, after two and half chapters of searing judgment, suddenly looks to another dimension of the day of the LORD—one of hope, joy and salvation. It is like seeing the rainbow of God's promise shining in the thunderclouds of God's judgment. The Israelites can rejoice, promised Zephaniah, as they look to the future, for their salvation is coming. God will save them. God will be with them. The resonance with the name of Jesus

(God is salvation) and Immanuel (God is with us) is very strong.

> Sing, O Daughter of Zion;
>   shout aloud, O Israel!
> Be glad and rejoice with all your heart,
>   O Daughter of Jerusalem!
> The LORD has taken away your punishment,
>   he has turned back your enemy.
> The LORD, the King of Israel, is with you;
>   never again will you fear any harm.
> On that day they will say to Jerusalem,
>   "Do not fear, O Zion;
>   do not let your hands hang limp.
> *The LORD your God is with you,*
>   *he is mighty to save.*
> He will take great delight in you,
>   he will quiet you with his love,
>   he will rejoice over you with singing." (Zeph 3:14-17, my italics)

Nor did Zephaniah confine this hope of future salvation to ethnic Israel alone. Like so many other prophets, he envisaged the nations also being drawn in to the purified unity of God's saved people in the future. As in so many places in the Old Testament, Israel is expanded to include the foreign nations who will come to God. Ethnic boundaries are dissolved, and God's people becomes a multinational community of all those who will call to the living God for salvation.

> Then will I purify the lips of the peoples,
>   that all of them may call on the name of the LORD
>   and serve him shoulder to shoulder. (Zeph 3:9)

Joel expresses the same confidence in words that inspired both Peter and Paul. When God pours out his Spirit on all people, then "everyone who calls on the name of the LORD will be saved" (Joel 2:32; see Acts 2:14-21; Rom 10:12-13).

And turning once more to the New Testament, we find that although of course our salvation has been accomplished by Christ on the cross (as a historical fact of the past), and although we are enjoying and living out the reality of it in the present, there is a sense in which we still look forward to our completed salvation in the future.

Our expectation of Jesus' return is actually our hope of the coming of our Savior, as Peter told his fellow Jews in Jerusalem.

> Repent, then, and turn to God, so that your sins may be wiped out, that times of refreshing may come from the Lord, and that he may send the Christ, who has been appointed for you—even Jesus. He must remain in heaven until the time comes for God to restore everything, as he promised long ago through his holy prophets. (Acts 3:19-21)

> Our citizenship is in heaven. And we eagerly await a Savior from there, the Lord Jesus Christ. (Phil 3:20)

Because the story of salvation is moving forward toward this great climax, Paul can urge believers to live in the light of their *future* salvation, as well as in the light of what they have *already* experienced.

> And do this [love your neighbor], understanding the present time. The hour has come for you to wake up from your slumber, because our salvation is nearer now than when we first believed. (Rom 13:11)

That will be the future day, guaranteed by all that Christ has already done, when we will finally be saved:

> Since we have now been justified by his blood, how much more *shall we be saved* from God's wrath through him! For if, when we were God's enemies, we were reconciled to him through the death of his Son, how much more, having been reconciled, *shall we be saved* through his life! (Rom 5:9-10, my italics)

Indeed, that will be the day when the totality of God's people, believing Jews and ingrafted Gentiles, will be saved. Paul's theology of mission, deeply rooted in the promises of the Old Testament, envisaged the Gentile nations being gathered in—actually "grafted in"—to the original olive tree—Old Testament Israel. But the result of that would be that Jews who were as yet unbelieving would be stirred by jealousy to turn to Jesus Christ and be grafted into their own olive tree. "And that is how all Israel will be saved" (Rom 11:26, my translation), says Paul as the climax of his argument in Romans 9—11. Notice that Paul does not say "that is *when*," but "that is *how*" (*houtōs*). Paul is not describing a *timetable* for the end of the world (as popularly misunderstood), but describing the *method* by which God is bringing about the salvation of his whole people, "all Israel." In that sense, it is a salvation as yet future. But when it is accomplished, then it will be the proof of God's ultimate faithfulness to his promise to Abraham and the universal climax of the covenant.

So when we hear that great doxology of the redeemed people of God in Revelation 7, we now know something of what they are celebrating when they cry out, "Salvation belongs to *our God*." They mean that salvation is the work of this biblical God, and that his saving work encompasses the whole of biblical covenantal history. To celebrate salvation is to retell that story, with hearts full of joy, gratitude and praise. For we are among those who have been saved, who are being saved and who will be saved, by the grace and power of God and the covenant blood of Christ.

Salvation: The Unique Story

The story other religions do not tell. This narrative nature of biblical salvation is the essence of its uniqueness.[2] That is to say, when the Bible talks about salvation, it is not talking about some generic common thing that all other religions also believe in, only in different ways. As soon as you mention salvation in the Bible you have to tell the story. And you have to tell *this* story—not any other. That's what makes the biblical understanding of salvation unique. For us as biblical Christians, salvation is not some mystical paradise in a celestial realm that all human beings hope to reach someday. Salvation is not an idea that all religions have in common and then aspire toward in their different ways. Salvation is not (as in the popular metaphor) something that waits for everybody at the summit of a mountain, which all religions climb toward from their different starting points—the implication being that any religion will get you to salvation in the end if you follow its path sincerely. This is a very popular opinion about religions (at least it is in the West among people who care about religion at all, and in India among tolerant Hindus), but it is far from the way the Bible talks about salvation.

All these notions of salvation start out from the wrong place—namely, that salvation is something we eventually hope to reach by our own religious efforts—with a little help from the gods or the gurus.[3] But as I said in chapter two, in the Bible God is the *subject,* not the *object,* of salvation. What that means is this. Salvation is the active work of God for us. God does it. God achieves it. God is the active subject. Salvation is not something that we have to work for, in order to persuade or manipulate God to let us have it. God is not the object of religious actions that we have to perform to get salvation for ourselves. God is the subject who has accomplished salvation for us. And, according to the Bible, he has accomplished it through the events recorded in this narrative history.

In the Bible, salvation is grounded in the "having-happened-ness" of the historical events by which God has acted to save humanity and creation. Salvation is what God has done already in the *past,* as a result of which certain outcomes are assured in the *future,* and because of which we live changed lives in the *present.* Salvation is not merely a hoped-for future toward which we may bend our religious efforts indefinitely, never sure whether we will get there until we do (or don't).

Biblical salvation makes statements about historically witnessed events and, on the basis of those facts, goes on to make equally affirmative statements about what God has achieved through them. Biblical salvation declares that God so loved the world that he gave his only Son. It affirms that God was in Christ reconciling the world to himself. It assures us that Christ died for our sins and was raised again on the third day for our justification. It asserts that God saved us, not because of any righteous things we had done, but because of his mercy. These are the great positive affirmations of biblical salvation, and they are all rooted and grounded in the biblical story itself.

Other religions do not save *because they do not tell this story.* They may have Scriptures and cultures of great antiquity, wisdom and dignity, and we should rightly respect all of those things. What I am saying here is not in any way meant to deride or dismiss the great depths of human reflection, literature, wisdom, culture, ethics, music, art and aspiration to be found within religious traditions and texts all over the world. But we are not talking about the human richness of religious traditions; rather, we are talking about whether they can be means of *salvation*—in the same sense that the Bible speaks of salvation. And my argument is that they cannot because other religions do not tell *this* story—the story of our covenant God and his saving action in history. They cannot therefore connect people to that story and to the Savior who is the great Subject of the story. They have no gospel to tell to the nations; they have no good news, for they do not know this story which alone constitutes the good news.

Is there salvation in other religions? This is the reason why, as Christians, we have to be very careful and clear if we are confronted with the question, "Is there salvation in other religions?" We need to ask what the questioner means before we can give an answer.

If the question means, "Is it possible that the living God, whom we know from the Bible, may save *people* who live in the context of other religions and may never hear about Jesus?" then that raises issues and possibilities about the destiny of the unevangelized that we will examine more carefully in chapter five. We may find reasons for optimism in answering that question, but they will come from within the Bible and through Christ, not from other religions as such.

If the question means, "Is there evidence in other religions of the revelation of God and of the grace of God—i.e., of the living, saving God of the Bible?" then we can surely answer yes. All human beings are made in the image of God and reflect something of the nature and character of God—however deformed. Religions, being human constructs, inevitably, therefore, embody something of that image of God also. Furthermore, God has revealed himself in and through creation itself and in the moral consciousness of all humanity. As sinners, we have distorted and suppressed this knowledge, but it is nevertheless a fact of human existence, as Paul argues in Romans 1. Paul could tell simple pagans in Lystra that "[God] has not left himself without testimony" among all the nations (Acts 14:17). And he could tell sophisticated pagans in Athens that God's desire is that "men would seek him and perhaps reach out for him and find him, though he is not far from each one of us" (Acts 17:27).

So there has been widespread willingness among many Christian theologians through the centuries to affirm the presence of God's general revelation, including even some awareness of his love, mercy and grace, within the contexts of the different religions of the world. This is understood as something we should attribute to the common grace of God and to the nature of humanity as created in God's image. All truth is God's truth. All truth and goodness flow from the character and grace of God. So wherever truth is found, or goodness practiced, we should affirm, not deny, the reality and presence of God in some way. If it were not for this common grace of God and his mercy even on the fallen sinful human race that we all belong to, life on earth would have become hell on earth long ago.

But if the question means, "Can *other religions as such* (i.e., as systems of worldview beliefs and practice) be means of salvation, in the same way and with the same effect as the salvation we find described in the Bible?" then the answer has to be a polite but firm no.

The reason we say no, denying that there is salvation is other religions, is *not* because other religions are inferior to Christianity *as a religion*. As we have already said, *religion* does not save anybody. It is not because Christianity is a good *religion,* or a better religion than others, that Christian believers are saved. We should avoid at all costs giving that impression, for it immediately parades an attitude of smug superiority, as if to say, "I've been saved because my religion is better than yours." That is the kind of arrogant, self-righteous hypocrisy that Jesus condemned and that the world rightly finds repulsive.

Salvation is to be found within the context of Christian faith and witness only because Christianity tells this story, whereas other religions do not. Salvation is contained *not* in Christianity as a religion (i.e., as a system, as an institution or even as a civilization), but in the story that Christians tell—in bearing witness to the biblical God and what God has done in history for our salvation. Salvation is guaranteed by and because of what God has done, not by our religious beliefs or practices.

You are my witnesses. This is also the reason why the primary stance that we take as Christians, when we talk about salvation, is one of *witness*. If salvation were something that we could find for ourselves or achieve through some self-chosen religious pathway, then evangelism would be a matter of going to other people and trying to persuade them to be like us, to follow our religious practices, or adhere to our sacred methods and rituals. We would be salesmen for our particular religious brand. We would be advertisers, making claims for our own particular product and promising happiness and satisfaction to those who buy this product instead of some other one. Sadly, that is how a lot of Christian evangelism actually does operate, and certainly it is what it often sounds like to the outside world. And understandably people reject such tactics.

But God did not call his people to persuade others to follow the practices of their religion in the hope of finding salvation for themselves. He did not call us to advertise our own brand or extend our own franchised salvation outlet stores. God called his people to be *witnesses* to what God himself has already done.

This is true in the Old Testament. The Israelites were surrounded by people who worshiped other gods. When they were in exile in Babylon, those other gods seemed extremely powerful. So how were other nations ever to come to know and worship the one true living God and be saved? By the Israelites bearing witness to what God had done and said. They were not to talk about their own *religion,* but to talk about the revealing and saving words and works of Yahweh, the God of Old Testament Israel. The LORD God would be the subject of their witness to the nations.

> All the nations gather together
> > and the peoples assemble.
> Which of them foretold this
> > and proclaimed to us the former things?
> Let them bring in their witnesses to prove they were right,
> > so that others may hear and say, "It is true."
> *"You are my witnesses,"* declares the LORD,
> > "and my servant whom I have chosen,
> so that you may know and believe me
> > and understand that I am he.
> Before me no god was formed,
> > nor will there be one after me.
> I, even I, am the LORD,
> > and apart from me there is no savior.
> I have revealed and saved and proclaimed—
> > I, and not some foreign god among you.
> *You are my witnesses,"*
> > declares the LORD, "that I am God." (Is 43:9-12, my italics)

Almost certainly, Jesus echoed this text when he laid the same responsibility of bearing witness on his disciples. Their mission was not to be the proponents of a new religion. They were not to be salesmen for a new philosophy, a freshly patented methodology for finding salvation, in a world already awash with all kinds of sects and cults offering whatever kind of salvation you wanted to buy. No, the disciples were simply to bear witness to what they had seen and heard in Jesus of Nazareth. They were to bear witness to his life, death and resurrection. They were to bear witness to his identity as the Son of the living God. They were to bear witness to what God had done through him, and what God now offers to the world in his name—forgiveness and salvation.

> Then he opened their minds so they could understand the Scriptures. He told them, "This is what is written: The Christ will suffer and rise from the dead on the third day, and repentance and forgiveness of sins will be preached in his name to all nations, beginning at Jerusalem. *You are witnesses of these things.* (Lk 24:45-48, my italics)

> But you will receive power when the Holy Spirit comes on you; and *you will be my witnesses* in Jerusalem, and in all Judea and Samaria, and to the ends of the earth. (Acts 1:8, my italics)

Of course, by stressing this stance of *witness* in relation to what God has done in salvation, I am not suggesting that all we have to do is to verbalize that witness. This is not just about *talk*. In both testaments, an utterly essential part of the witness that God's people must bear to the salvation he has accomplished for them is the evidence of transformed *living*. Witness is ethical, not merely verbal.

In the Old Testament, the scorching critique of the prophets was that the Israelites were failing utterly in their mandate of bearing witness to Yahweh precisely because they were failing to live according to Yahweh's laws and standards. This applied right across the range of their practical life—from personal morality through sexual ethics, family relationships, financial dealings, truth and honesty, agricultural justice, judicial integrity, and right up to political leadership and international relations. A people that would not *walk* in the ways of the LORD could bear no *witness* to the ways of the LORD. Most of the prophets brought this challenge, but Ezekiel probably focused his searchlight on it more ruthlessly than all. The Israelites, far from being any kind of witness to the nations by the quality of their life and society, had sunk below the level of the pagan nations that surrounded them.

> This is what the Sovereign LORD says: This is Jerusalem, which I have set

in the center of the nations, with countries all around her. Yet in her wickedness she has rebelled against my laws and decrees more than the nations and countries around her. She has rejected my laws and has not followed my decrees.

Therefore this is what the Sovereign LORD says: You have been more unruly than the nations around you and have not followed my decrees or kept my laws. You have not even conformed to the standards of the nations around you. (Ezek 5:5-7)

And in the New Testament, the plain teaching of Jesus and the apostles, the only kind of witness that is worthy of the gospel and that has any chance of being effective, is the witness which is borne through the shining light of good deeds and Christlike, self-giving love.

> You are the light of the world. A city on a hill cannot be hidden. Neither do people light a lamp and put it under a bowl. Instead they put it on its stand, and it gives light to everyone in the house. In the same way, let your light shine before men, that they may see your good deeds and praise your Father in heaven. (Mt 5:14-16)

> By this all men will know that you are my disciples, if you love one another. (Jn 13:35)

> Teach [Christian] slaves to be subject to their masters in everything, to try to please them, not to talk back to them, and not to steal from them, but to show that they can be fully trusted, so that in every way they will make the teaching about God our Savior attractive. (Tit 2:9-10)

Mahatma Gandhi is reputed to have said that if the Christians in India were to live like Jesus (to whose teaching and example Gandhi was much attracted), then there would be no Hindus. But of course what Gandhi meant was that there was in fact such a credibility gap between what Jesus taught and lived out, on the one hand, and the lives of his alleged followers, on the other hand, that Christianity itself did not have the conversionary power that it could have if the Christian message were matched by Christian living.

No other Scriptures. The fact that salvation is rooted in the biblical story is also the reason why we must resist the suggestion, popular in some quarters, that we may substitute the Scriptures of other faiths for the Old Testament. The argument goes like this: People sometimes find that their previous religion prepares the way for them to find faith in Christ. Christ fulfills the longings that their previous religion and its Scriptures had planted in them (I have Indian Christian friends who have told me this). So if that is true in some way, then (it is said) we may allow those Scriptures of other religions to function as a culturally appropriate alternative to the Old Testament, as a preparation for Jesus. The Old Testament prepared for Jesus in the Jewish world of his day. The Scriptures of other faiths can prepare for Jesus in the cultural world of those other religions.

But this is very dangerous and mistaken. It ignores the necessity of the Old Testament as the Scriptures which tell the story and declare the promise that lead up to Jesus. Jesus only makes sense in the light of the Old Testament Scriptures. These were the Scriptures which provided Jesus' sense of identity and mission.[4] These were the Scriptures with which the early Christians went out into the world of their own day (not just the Jewish world, but also the Greek and Roman world). Once they learned to read the Old Testament in the light of Jesus the Messiah (as he told them to do, Lk 24:44-47), the followers of Jesus used them pervasively in their mission. The apostles were planting, nurturing and teaching churches using the Old Testament Scriptures long before the New Testament documents were written. From Paul's earliest letters (1 Thessalonians, Galatians), it is clear that he had been teaching them the roots of their Christian faith in the Old Testament very thoroughly.

Without the Old Testament, the story of Jesus and of salvation loses its beginning, its sense of direction and its ultimate plot. No, a biblical perspective on salvation needs the perspective of the *whole* Bible. For the whole canon of Scripture was generated, informed and shaped by the saving acts of God that reached their central climax in the life, death and resurrection of Jesus. Whatever previous religious faith and experience may be there in the journey that any person makes to faith in Jesus as Lord and Savior, it is essential that that person's worldview, life, experience, personal story, is from then on re-centered on the truly biblical Jesus, so that it is the biblical Jesus that now takes root within his or her mind and culture, transforming and converting both to Christ—not merely molding Christ into the unreconstructed shape of the surrounding culture.

A vigorous, village-level church-planting movement in North India, with whose leaders I have had some limited involvement, stresses very strongly the need to teach even the simplest new believers the whole Bible story, including the core narrative of the Old Testament. So those who plan the training of new church planters and the young-in-faith new pastors of small groups of believers give a lot of time to inculcating "the story of redemption." It is not enough for them merely to know some key Bible verses, unrelated to anything. Rather, the leaders drill them in the whole outline story of the Bible, with its four great movements of creation, fall, redemption in history and new creation. One leader said to me, "We are about the business of 'myth-replacement.' Hindus derive their worldview from their great myths and stories of Ram and Krishna, etc. We need to make new believers so familiar with the great story of the Bible *as a whole* that it replaces that old Hindu worldview, because they are now living and working out of the biblical narrative. So we teach them the whole Bible framework, as well as the deeper content of particular books." It seems to me that such an approach will lead to Christian communities that are growing, not merely in numbers but also in depth and strength. They will have a biblically rooted and informed understanding of what their salvation actually is and means. And it seems to me that such an approach clearly reflects the missionary practice of Paul himself.

QUESTIONS FOR REFLECTION OR DISCUSSION

1. "The covenant with Abraham links our understanding of salvation both to our ecclesiology and to our missiology." Discuss the implications of this statement. How has this chapter strengthened the connection in your mind between your doctrine of salvation on the one hand, and your view of the church and of mission on the other?

2. When you tell the story of salvation, do you only tell the story of the cross? Why is this biblically inadequate, even though the cross is central? How should the Bible's whole covenantal narrative of salvation affect the way we do our ministry and engage in evangelism?

3. Do you agree that it is possible to affirm that other religions contain elements of truth and goodness, and yet at the same time to deny that they can be ways of salvation? For what reasons can we affirm the one while denying the other? What difference does this make to how we relate to people of other faiths?

4. "In both testaments, an utterly essential part of the witness that God's people must bear to the salvation he has accomplished for them is the evidence of transformed *living*. Witness is ethical, not merely verbal. . . . A people that would not *walk* in the ways of the LORD could bear no *witness* to the ways of the LORD." What is the state of the witness of the church in your context? Does it reflect the state of the church's "walk"—its ethical obedience to God? How can you help people to keep these two things together in thought and practice?

5

Salvation and
Our Experience

Salvation belongs to our God,
who sits on the throne,
and to the Lamb. (Rev 7:10)

WE ARE EXPLORING THIS WONDERFUL VERSE AS OUR CONTROL TEXT. But
we must not treat it merely as a line in a creed or statement of faith. This
is not a dull piece of ritual or a monotone recitation.

We are told that John saw a vast crowd of people, waving palm
branches and crying this out in a loud voice. The declaration of Revelation 7:10 is immediately followed by a great doxology from the angels, elders and living creatures of John's vision. In other words, *this is
a celebration!* This is the song of those who have been saved. It is a celebration of the *experience* of salvation. This is the testimony of those
who know what it is to be saved by God, and who want the whole universe to know.

So in this chapter we turn to salvation as a matter of experience. We
shall think first of how salvation is to be received and experienced for
oneself, and then secondly of how the Bible portrays salvation being mediated to others through successive generations.

EXPERIENCING SALVATION

When God saves you, you know it! The covenantal relationship with the saving God of the Bible was, and is, meant to be experienced and enjoyed by God's people. Salvation is a matter of celebrated experience. Celebration of salvation in the Bible had different flavors.

- Sometimes it means celebrating some *recent personal testimony* of how God has acted in salvation (as in so many psalms).

- Sometimes it means celebrating the *collective historical memory* of the great saving events which constitute our knowledge of God as Savior (such as the exodus in the Old Testament, or the cross in the New Testament).

- Sometimes it means celebrating *in advance* the salvation to which we look forward, through engaging our faith imagination in worship.

Because salvation in the Bible is always connected to the covenant between God and his people, it is experienced through our relationships in both directions. That is to say, we experience salvation through faith in God. But we also experience salvation along with all God's people—with all those who know him as "our God," all those whom he has saved and will save. Salvation, in other words, is a matter of believing *and* belonging—believing in the God who saves us, and belonging to the people God is saving.

Salvation is experienced through faith. Salvation belongs to our God and is therefore a matter of God's initiative and God's power. For that reason, salvation is experienced on our side simply through trusting reception. God has done it. We receive it. This is already clear from our earlier point that, in the Bible, nothing and nobody else can save except God. We certainly cannot save ourselves. Therefore, if there is to be salvation at all, it must come from God and be received from him in faith. We contribute nothing to it. In the matter of salvation, the familiar English proverb, "God helps those who help themselves," is the exact opposite of the truth: On the contrary, as William Temple said, "All is of God; the only

thing of my very own which I contribute to my redemption is the sin
from which I need to be redeemed."[1]

In the Old Testament, we often read of the cry for help, sometimes
from individuals, sometimes from the whole nation. This is a clear ac-
ceptance of one's own inability and need of rescue. Alongside that, salvation is experienced through repentance (turning away from sin and
rebellion and back toward God—a favorite theme of Jeremiah) and
through responsive loving fear and obedience toward God.

The salvation of God, says the psalmist, is for those who *call* on God,
fear him, *cry* to him and *love* him—and these are all part of what it means
to trust him. Salvation comes by faith.

> The LORD is near to all who call on him,
> to all who call on him in truth.
> He fulfills the desires of those who fear him;
> he hears their cry and *saves* them.
> The LORD watches over all who love him,
> but all the wicked he will destroy. (Ps 145:18-20, my italics)

Isaiah, whose name means, "Yahweh saves," has a developed understanding of God's salvation, and it is wholly dependent on humble, repentant faith.

> Surely this is our God;
> we trusted in him, and he saved us. (Is 25:9)

> In repentance and rest is your salvation,
> in quietness and trust is your strength. (Is 30:15)

And everywhere in the New Testament, of course, salvation is offered
by God's grace only on the basis of repentance and faith. Perhaps the
classic text comes in Ephesians, where Paul makes it crystal clear that we
can do no good work that will provide any grounds for our salvation; but
having been saved by God's grace through faith, we are indeed committed by God himself to live lives of good works.

But because of his great love for us, God, who is rich in mercy, made us alive with Christ even when we were dead in transgressions—it is by grace you have been saved. And God raised us up with Christ and seated us with him in the heavenly realms in Christ Jesus, in order that in the coming ages he might show the incomparable riches of his grace, expressed in his kindness to us in Christ Jesus. For it is by grace you have been saved, through faith—and this not from yourselves, it is the gift of God—not by works, so that no one can boast. For we are God's workmanship, created in Christ Jesus to do good works, which God prepared in advance for us to do. (Eph 2:4-10)

We are saved *by* grace, through faith; we are saved not *by* good works, but *unto* good works.

The distinctive heart of the biblical gospel, distinctive, that is, from other religious systems, is that salvation is not something we achieve but something we can only receive. And faith is the means of receiving.

Even faith is seen as a gift of God in the New Testament. When Gentiles first turned to Christ, the earliest disciples saw this as a gift of God's grace also. Peter described to the disciples back in Jerusalem how Cornelius and his family had come to faith, and they rejoiced with him in this manifest act of God:

"As I began to speak, the Holy Spirit came on them as he had come on us at the beginning. Then I remembered what the Lord had said: 'John baptized with water, but you will be baptized with the Holy Spirit.' So *if God gave them the same gift* as he gave us, who believed in the Lord Jesus Christ, who was I to think that I could oppose God?"

When they heard this, they had no further objections and praised God, saying, "So then, *God has granted* even the Gentiles repentance unto life." (Acts 11:15-18, my italics)

In saying that faith is a gift of God, we are not saying that it is not also *our* faith—i.e., faith that we deliberately exercise. We do make the decision to trust in Christ, but we must never think of faith as some kind of good deed by which we earn our salvation. We are saved by God's grace *through* trusting; we are not saved merely *by* trusting in and of itself—as if we had faith in our own faith.

When a firefighter comes to rescue you from a burning building, you gladly trust him or her to carry you out. You are saved through very sensibly deciding to trust the firefighter. But it is the firefighter who saves you, with strength and courage. You are saved *by* the firefighter's strength, *through* your faith in him or her. In the same way, we are saved *by* God's grace (for God does the saving), *through* our faith (for we do the trusting).

Salvation is experienced along with God's people. Because salvation is covenantal, we are saved as part of the people of God as a whole. Our faith connects us to the story of God's saving action among that people. So of course we must know that story of salvation. In order to believe it, we must know it. To know it, we must hear it. This is the sequence that Paul has in mind. First of all, he quotes from Joel 2:32, "Everyone who calls on the name of the Lord *will be saved.*" But then he goes on to ask, "How, then, can they call on the one they have not believed in? And how can they believe in the one of whom they have not heard?" (Rom 10:14, my italics).

These questions applied, of course, as much to Israelites in the Old Testament (as Paul does so apply them) as to the Gentiles. Whether for Jews or Gentiles, salvation comes through knowing and trusting in what God has done for our salvation, which of course now means the life, death and resurrection of the Messiah, Jesus. We need to know the story of Jesus and trust in his saving work. But that story is itself the climax of the great story of redemption in the Old Testament.

This is the reason why there is such an emphasis on the constant teaching of the great traditions of Israel's faith in the Old Testament. Through knowing these stories and teachings, the Israelites were called to love, trust and obey their covenantal God, and in that way to appropriate the blessing of his saving acts on their behalf. The saving God must be *known*. And he was known through the story of salvation.

After retelling the story of how God had delivered the people of Israel from Egypt and then protected them in their travels through the wilderness, and revealed his name and his law to them at Sinai, Moses comments, "You were shown these things so that you might *know* that the LORD is God; besides him there is no other" (Deut 4:35, my italics). They were to know God through knowing The Story. They must tell and retell the story of the exodus. That was how they would know Yahweh as the saving God, and thereby experience his salvation for themselves.

Likewise, Christians must tell and retell the story of the cross and resurrection. The writers of the Gospels devoted more of the costly parchment of the Gospels to the events of Jesus' death and resurrection than to any other part of Jesus' life. There are four Gospels, and each gives surprisingly extended space to the last week of Jesus' life, the days of his death and his resurrection. It is very clear what they wanted us to hear for our salvation. Salvation is through faith, and "faith comes from hearing the message, and the message is heard through the word of Christ" (Rom 10:17).

So our experience of salvation is not just a private ticket to heaven. We are not saved by being picked off one by one by God and whisked off to our private paradise. We are saved by entering into the story of salvation along with all God's people, knowing ourselves to be among the people whom God has chosen, called, redeemed and covenanted.

MEDIATING SALVATION

Mediated through the Scriptures. So, as we have seen, the *story* of salvation is crucial. God has acted to save his people, and his people need to know the facts. But how? This leads us to the key role of the Scriptures in mediating salvation. For it is in the Bible that we have the record of those saving events. Here we have in our hands the testimony of those who experienced the saving events at first hand. In the Old Testament, that means the generation of the exodus. In the New Testament, it means those who witnessed the life, death and resurrection of Jesus. These were the people who had firsthand experience of the saving acts of God. They saw them, they lived at the same time, they were direct witnesses.

But what about the generations who followed? What about all the rest of us? How do *we* enter into the experience of a salvation that is so clearly rooted in unique historical events? If salvation is what only God can do and actually has done, and if what God has done for salvation was "once for all" in history, how can anybody else be saved who was not actually there at the time?

This question, in fact, is as old as the story itself. The people to whom Deuteronomy addressed the words "*you* were shown these things so that you might know" (Deut 4:35, my italics) had *not* actually been shown them. At least, not as adults. The audience of the speeches in Deuteronomy was the next generation after the exodus. For them, as for us, it was a matter of knowing the story. Then, from knowing the story, they needed to know what it proved about God. And then they needed to know and respond to the God revealed to them in that story.

So it is also for us. We receive salvation by knowing the story of Jesus—his life, death and resurrection. Then we understand what that story proves about God—his wrath against sin and his love for sinners. Then we come to trust in the God to whom the story testifies, and to see that it is *our* story—in the sense that it was *for us,* not merely for those who first experienced and witnessed it.

> We may not know, we cannot tell
>   What pains he had to bear;
> But we believe it was for us
>   He hung and suffered there.[2]

> I have been crucified with Christ and I no longer live, but Christ lives in me. The life I live in the body, I live by faith in the Son of God, *who loved me and gave himself for me.* (Gal 2:20, my italics)

It is through the Scriptures that we come to know the story itself, to know the meaning of the story and to know the God of the story. Only in the Bible do we have this great portrayal of the saving work of God. Only in the Bible, therefore, do we have the primary and indispensable tool through which the salvation that God has accomplished is mediated to those who so desperately need it.

This explains the great emphasis on *the word* in relation to the gospel of salvation in the New Testament. This is definitely not because salvation is a conceptual, abstract or systematized verbal philosophy. Salvation does not consist in *mere* words, in that sense. Rather, words are needed because salvation is a narrative that needs to be told. Salvation is good news that needs to be announced, about events that need to be known, revealing a God who needs to be trusted.

So Jesus warned that if the *word* were snatched away by the devil, then hearers would not believe and thus be saved (Lk 8:12). John observes that the Scriptures, along with the Father and John the Baptist, testify to Jesus, in order that people who search them may have life—one of John's primary salvation terms (Jn 5:31-40). Paul reminds the Corinthians of the basic Easter story ("according to the Scriptures") and then tells them, "by this gospel [i.e., faith-generating knowledge of these events] you are saved" (1 Cor 15:2). Even the Old Testament Scriptures, Paul reminded Timothy, "are able to make you wise for salvation through faith in Christ [the Messiah] Jesus" (2 Tim 3:15). Why? Because they tell the essential story of this saving God, a story that reaches its climax in Jesus Christ, the Savior.

Biblical salvation, then, is inseparable from the biblical word—the Scriptures themselves. Salvation is not a purely subjective experience of esoteric faith and individual piety. Salvation is rather a *biblically informed* experience. Salvation means entering into *this* story of *this* God saving the world through *these* events, and ultimately through *this* person, his Son, the Messiah, Jesus of Nazareth. It is the Bible that mediates this salvation to us, and there is no other.

This is why there can be no substitute for the faithful preaching and teaching of the Bible. It is the word of life. It is the prime means by which

God brings people to salvation, through the knowledge of what he has done to save them.

Mediated through the sacraments. Another way in which our experience of salvation is mediated is not only through the Scriptures but also through the sacraments that are recorded and commanded in Scripture. The sacraments remain secondary to the word of Scripture itself. But they are important means of communicating and embracing the meaning of salvation. The story of salvation is not merely to be recollected. It is to be reenacted in such a way as to connect each generation with the living power of the original events themselves. Of course, this does not mean that we somehow do it again, as if we were contributing our own piece of religious magic power to the process of getting salvation. No, God has done it, once and for all, with no need for any repetition or topping up. However, by the dramatic actions of the sacraments, we make those once-for-all events live again for us in the present.

For Israel, of course, the major sacrament of salvation was the annual Passover. In this family feast, Israelites (and Jews still today) would relive the story of the exodus. They feel the pain of the slavery and hard labor. They hear the liberating promises of God through Moses. They shudder at the hammer blows of the plagues upon the Egyptians. They give thanks for the blood of the Passover lambs that spared their own firstborn from death. They gasp at the hurried nighttime flight from Egypt. They celebrate the great deliverance by God at the Sea of Reeds. This is the story of salvation for Israel, and it was to be relived every year at the same time.

The two biblical Christian sacraments are baptism and the Lord's Supper (or Holy Communion or Eucharist). Both embody the story of salvation, though the second does so much more explicitly.

Baptism, corresponding to circumcision in the Old Testament, is the ceremony of initiation into, and inclusion within, the covenant community of God's people through Christ. In several ways, in the New Testament, it is linked to the essential biblical story of salvation.

In him you were also circumcised, in the putting off of the sinful nature, not with a circumcision done by the hands of men but with the circumcision done by Christ, having been buried with him in baptism and raised with him through your faith in the power of God, who raised him from the dead. (Col 2:11-12)

Paul here links Christian baptism with circumcision, thus connecting us to the original story of Abraham (whom God commanded to circumcise his descendants as a sign of belonging within the covenant, Gen 17). But Paul says that now, for us, our identification with Christ is a spiritual circumcision, which is effected by our baptism. Then he portrays baptism itself as a symbolic reenactment of the death, burial and resurrection of Jesus. By going into or under the water of baptism, we die with him. By coming out of the water of baptism, we rise to new life with him. In this sense, the sacrament tells the story of salvation, for those who are taught its meaning (as Paul clearly had taught his churches). And those who thus enter into the story of salvation through baptism must live a new life henceforth.

Shall we go on sinning so that grace may increase? By no means! We died to sin; how can we live in it any longer? Or don't you know that all of us who were baptized into Christ Jesus were baptized into his death? We were therefore buried with him through baptism into death in order that, just as Christ was raised from the dead through the glory of the Father, we too may live a new life. (Rom 6:1-4)

Elsewhere, Paul compared the early experience of Old Testament Israel with baptism. Speaking of the great story of the exodus and the crossing of the Sea of Reeds, led by the cloud of God's presence, Paul makes the parallel in this way:

For I do not want you to be ignorant of the fact, brothers, that our forefathers were all under the cloud and that they all passed through the sea. They were all baptized into Moses in the cloud and in the sea. (1 Cor 10:1-2)

Other aspects of the symbolism of baptism are of course dependent on the story of the cross—such as that we are cleansed from sin (as water washes the body) and are made alive through regeneration (as water gives life). Both aspects are mentioned in Titus 3:5, which probably has baptism in mind.

The Lord's Supper, however, is the sacrament that most clearly retells the story of salvation. Not only does it actually tell the story of the atoning passion of Christ, but also, because it was initiated in the context of the Passover, it links the New Testament story of the cross to the Old Testament story of the exodus—thus combining for us the whole biblical narrative of salvation into a single dramatic (yet essentially very simple) action.

So, as Jesus said, every time we eat the bread and drink the wine, we do it in remembrance of him. Now it is common enough in human experience to hold memorial services. But the normal feature of any memorial event is to celebrate some person's *life*. We recall their *life story* and the things they said and did. What is remarkable and unique about the Christian memorial of Jesus—our sacrament of Holy Communion—is that it focuses exclusively on his *death*. For it is in the death of Jesus Christ that we have salvation, the forgiveness of sins. It is the story of the cross that we must tell, above all, in the sacrament of salvation. He gave his body, he shed his blood. And he did so for us and for many, for the remission of sins. This is what we remember and declare every time we take the bread and drink the cup.

These sacraments are more than just memorials of the events they celebrate. When we engage in celebrating the sacrament, we enter a kind of two-way time machine. First of all, this sacramental time machine lands us down in the biblical word itself. Every generation of Israelites and Jews says of themselves, "We were slaves of Pharaoh in Egypt, but the LORD brought us out" (e.g., Deut 6:21). Every Christian hears the words of Jesus on the night of the Last Supper as addressed to him or herself: "This is my body, given for *you*." It is as if we were there, experiencing these things along with those who were actually there physically. The sacrament, as it were, dissolves the walls of history and lets us step back into that moment of saving action. "Were you there when they crucified my Lord?" sings the familiar African-American spiritual. Sacramentally, and theologically, we are able to answer yes.

On the other hand the sacrament brings up the past events as if they were now. The sacramental time machine brings the effect and power of the original, unrepeatable and once-for-all saving act of God out of the past and into our present lives. The story lives again in our imagination and faith. Israelites experienced afresh the liberation of exodus. Christians feel once again the grace and cleansing blood of the cross and give thanks for its power in the present.

In the Anglican service of Holy Communion, the words that are spoken as each person receives the bread and wine express both the past and the present aspect of the sacrament.

Taking us back to *the past:*

> The body of Christ that was given for you. . . . The blood of Christ that was shed for you. . . .
> Take and eat this in remembrance that Christ died for you. . . . Drink this in remembrance that Christ's blood was shed for you.

And bringing the effects of Christ's death into *our present:*

> And feed on him [now] in your heart by faith with thanksgiving. . . . And be thankful.

And there is even a sense in which the Communion service directs our thoughts to the future also, for Paul tells us that "whenever you eat this bread and drink this cup, you proclaim the Lord's death *until he comes"* (1 Cor 11:26), possibly reflecting on the words of Jesus, "I will not drink again of the fruit of the vine until the kingdom of God comes" (Lk 22:18). So our sacramental time machine transports us forward also in anticipation of the day when the Lord returns and our salvation is complete.

So then, for us as believers, our experience of salvation is mediated to us through our reading and hearing the words of Scripture, and through participating in the sacraments that celebrate the saving work of God. The Bible tells the story. The sacraments reenact it. We put our faith in the God revealed in the story, and we trust in what he has done to save us. And we renew our faith regularly by participating in the sacraments as "means of grace." This does not imply, of course, that the sacraments are mechanical grace providers. God's grace is received by faith in Christ, as we "feed on him in [our] hearts by faith with thanksgiving." The sacraments are not what save us, in and of themselves. They are signs, pointing to the God who saves us by his grace. The sacraments *focus* our faith, reminding us of the saving events in which our faith is grounded and the saving Person in whom our faith is placed.

THE ASSURANCE OF SALVATION

It's all very well, we might think, for the saints in glory in John's vision in Revelation to celebrate and sing about salvation: they are enjoying it already! But what about the rest of us? What about here and now? Can we rejoice in the same way—not because we have already received all there is to possess of the salvation God has accomplished for us, but because we can be absolutely certain of doing so? Can we be sure? Can we have, in the older language of Christian devotion, "assurance of salvation"? Undoubtedly the Bible answers, "Yes, we can."

Assurance comes from the objectivity of the story. The first foundation for our assurance of salvation is the one that this book has been stressing all along. Salvation is not something we ourselves do, feel, think, wish for or achieve. If it were, then we might rightly doubt whether we have ever done enough to be sure of being saved. Or we might worry that we don't feel saved. But the Bible makes it clear that salvation is something that God has accomplished. That means our salvation is grounded in the objectivity of the story. By *objectivity*, I mean something that stands outside and independent of ourselves.

The story of salvation in the Bible is a story of historical facts and events. There is a "having-happened-ness" about them, which is there whether or not I choose to believe in them. God chose and called Abraham; God delivered Israel from Egypt; God sent his Son into the world; Jesus of Nazareth was born, lived and died on the cross; God raised him from the dead. In these events, as Paul says, "God was reconciling the world to himself in Christ" (2 Cor 5:19). That is why the Apostles' Creed, summarizing the essence of Christian faith, emphasizes the historical facts. "Jesus Christ . . . born of the virgin Mary, suffered under Pontius Pilate, was crucified, died and was buried."

So assurance of salvation comes not from trusting in my own faith for its own sake, but rather from trusting in the object of my faith—what God has actually done to make my salvation possible.

Using a previous illustration: if you need to be rescued from a building on fire, you can have assurance of your salvation by the objective facts. The fire engine has come. The ladder has been put against the building. The ladder has been stretched up to reach the window where you are stranded. The firefighter has climbed up the ladder. The firefighter is now at your window offering to rescue you. Those facts of life-saving rescue are objectively there, whether you take advantage of them or not. Of course you would be mad *not* to take advantage of the facts by trusting the firefighter; but the facts are objectively there whether you trust him or not. The means of salvation is accomplished, and when you exercise faith and let the firefighter carry you, you can be sure of your salvation from then on.

Suppose you could go back to the Old Testament and ask an Israelite farmer if he was saved and how he could be sure. He would sit you down for a while and tell you a story—or rather, *the* story of God's deliverance of his people and gift of the land. These were the monumental, tangible, objective facts which constituted his knowledge of redemption. Listen to what the farmer was instructed to say, every year. Here is an affirmation of salvation, which positively rings with assurance and joy—all based on historical facts. This is what I mean by saying that our assurance rests in the objectivity of the story of salvation.

> When you have entered the land the LORD your God is giving you as an inheritance and have taken possession of it and settled in it, take some of the firstfruits of all that you produce from the soil of the land the LORD your God is giving you and put them in a basket. Then go to the place the LORD your God will choose as a dwelling for his Name and say to the priest in office at the time, "I declare today to the LORD your God that I have come to the land the LORD swore to our forefathers to give us." The priest shall take the basket from your hands and set it down in front of the altar of the LORD your God. Then you shall declare before the LORD your God: "My father was a wandering Aramean, and he went down into Egypt with a few people and lived there and became a great nation, powerful and numerous. But the Egyptians mistreated us and made us suffer, putting us to hard labor. Then we cried out to the LORD, the God of our fathers, and the LORD heard our voice and saw our misery, toil and oppression. So the LORD brought us out of Egypt with a mighty hand and an outstretched arm, with great terror and with miraculous signs and wonders. He brought us to this place and gave us this land, a land flowing with milk and honey; and now I bring the firstfruits of the soil that you, O LORD, have given me." Place the basket before the LORD your God and bow down before him. And you and the Levites and the aliens among you shall rejoice in all the good things the LORD your God has given to you and your household. (Deut 26:1-11)

Paul was faced with a failure of confidence in the church at Corinth. People were worried about the resurrection of some Christians who had died, or indeed questioned their own future resurrection. There was a loss of assurance. Paul counters this with a very strong series of arguments that run through 1 Corinthians 15, but it is noticeable that he starts in the same place, in principle, as the Israelite farmer, by reciting the facts on which salvation is based—namely (in New Testament terms, of course), the gospel facts of the death and resurrection of Jesus. And significantly, he says, "*by this gospel you are saved,* if you hold firmly to the word I preached to you." That is: the facts of the gospel are there; it is the facts of the gospel that make your salvation possible; it is the facts of the gospel you must hold onto for your assurance and hope. Here is how Paul himself puts it:

> Now, brothers, I want to remind you of the gospel I preached to you, which you received and on which you have taken your stand. By this gospel you are saved, if you hold firmly to the word I preached to you. Otherwise, you have believed in vain.
>
> For what I received I passed on to you as of first importance: that Christ died for our sins according to the Scriptures, that he was buried, that he was raised on the third day according to the Scriptures, and that he appeared to Peter, and then to the Twelve. After that, he appeared to more than five hundred of the brothers at the same time. (1 Cor 15:1-6)

Assurance comes from the promises of God. A second major source of assurance of salvation comes from remembering the words of our control text: "salvation belongs to *our God.*" And our God is the God who has made "exceeding great and precious promises" (2 Pet 1:4 KJV). So assurance comes from knowing the God of the promises, and trusting in the promises of God.

This was certainly the case in the Old Testament. Abraham, of course, is the great model of trust in the promise of God—matching his faith with his obedience. How could Abraham be so sure? Hebrews points out to us that God not only made a promise, but he based it on God's own self—through the form of an oath on his own existence. God's promises are as secure as God's existence! God cannot fail to keep his word without ceasing to be God. And if the second is unthinkable, so is the first. So, says Hebrews,

> When God made his promise to Abraham, since there was no one greater for him to swear by, he swore by himself, saying, "I will surely bless you

and give you many descendants." And so after waiting patiently, Abraham received what was promised.

Men swear by someone greater than themselves, and the oath confirms what is said and puts an end to all argument. Because God wanted to make the unchanging nature of his purpose very clear to the heirs of what was promised, he confirmed it with an oath. God did this so that, by two unchangeable things in which it is impossible for God to lie, we who have fled to take hold of the hope offered to us may be greatly encouraged. We have this hope as an anchor for the soul, firm and secure. (Heb 6:13-19)

And you notice how the writer to the Hebrews makes the example of Abraham relevant to us by saying at the end of that passage that *we too* can have the same rock-solid security in our faith because of the character and promise of God.

And Hebrews 11, of course, puts alongside Abraham many other great men and women of faith—named and unnamed—in the Old Testament whose faith in God's promises gave them assurance of the salvation they had not yet seen. Assurance comes from faith in God's promise.

Some of the most powerful psalms are those that express trust in God's promise—even when things seemed desperate. There are many, but my favorite is Psalm 27, because it breathes assurance of salvation on the basis of trusting in the person, character and promise of God.

> The LORD is my light and my salvation—
>   whom shall I fear?
> The LORD is the stronghold of my life—
>   of whom shall I be afraid? . . .
> I am still confident of this:
>   I will see the goodness of the LORD
>   in the land of the living. (Ps 27:1, 13)

In the New Testament, the apostles repeatedly urge their readers to have full confidence in God's promise, and in that way to thoroughly enjoy the assurance of salvation. Peter, for example, speaks of how we are

kept by God's power for our salvation, while our salvation is being kept
for us in heaven: we are doubly "kept," and therefore doubly assured. We
have, says Peter,

> an inheritance that can never perish, spoil or fade—kept in heaven for
> you, who through faith are shielded by God's power until the coming of
> the salvation that is ready to be revealed in the last time. (1 Pet 1:4-5)

For this reason, we can be fully assured while we wait, believing in
the Christ we have not seen, and therefore confident of the salvation that
is ours:

> Though you have not seen him, you love him; and even though you do
> not see him now, you believe in him and are filled with an inexpressible
> and glorious joy, for you are receiving the goal of your faith, the salvation
> of your souls. (1 Pet 1:8-9)

Probably the best-known classic text on assurance of salvation comes
at the end of Romans 8, based on all Paul has argued about the faithfulness of God to his promise and all that he has accomplished in Christ to
fulfill that promise.

> And we know that in all things God works for the good of those who love
> him, who have been called according to his purpose. For those God fore-
> knew he also predestined to be conformed to the likeness of his Son, that
> he might be the firstborn among many brothers. And those he predes-
> tined, he also called; those he called, he also justified; those he justified,
> he also glorified.
>
> Who shall separate us from the love of Christ? Shall trouble or hard-
> ship or persecution or famine or nakedness or danger or sword? As it is
> written:
>
> > "For your sake we face death all day long;
> >   we are considered as sheep to be slaughtered."
>
> No, in all these things we are more than conquerors through him who
> loved us. For I am convinced that neither death nor life, neither angels

nor demons, neither the present nor the future, nor any powers, neither height nor depth, nor anything else in all creation, will be able to separate us from the love of God that is in Christ Jesus our Lord. (Rom 8:28-30, 35-39)

Assurance comes from the witness and work of the Holy Spirit. It would be unfortunate if the previous two sections gave the impression that assurance of salvation was only a matter of knowing some objective facts and believing some divine promises—as if it were all only in our heads, as a matter of cognitive assent to certain statements. Is there nothing that we can actually feel, subjectively, for ourselves? Is there not also a profoundly personal, internal, emotional and spiritual *experience* of salvation? Am I not actually also supposed to *feel* saved? And of course the answer is a resounding and joyful "Yes!"

It has been very important in the previous sections to stress the objective nature of biblical salvation, precisely because so many popular ideas think only about inner, personal or mystical dimensions when they talk about salvation. But, as I have said, you don't get rescued from a burning building just by feeling safe subjectively; you are saved only by trusting in what the firefighters do to save you. Salvation is based not on feelings but on facts. It is good and desirable to feel saved, but we are not saved by feeling saved! We are saved by what God has done. Nevertheless, there is certainly an inner, personal, subjective side to salvation too, and the Bible has plenty to say about it.

This is where the Bible emphasizes the role of the Holy Spirit in salvation. I have already mentioned that repentance and faith are described in the New Testament as the gifts of God's grace. Both are associated with the Holy Spirit. Jesus said that it would be the work of the Holy Spirit to convict people of "guilt in regard to sin and righteousness" (Jn 16:8-10). And the gift of faith in Jesus in Acts is accompanied by the gift of the Holy Spirit (e.g., Acts 10:44-48; 11:15-18). So the work of the Holy Spirit is to convince people of the truth of the gospel, and to make real in their hearts the right response to the good news about Jesus, so that people can come into the experience of salvation.

Then, once we have come into that new relationship with God through Christ, it is the Holy Spirit who bears witness within our own minds and hearts that it has indeed happened—that we have indeed been born again and have become children of God. God has made us sons and heirs,[3] objectively. But it is the Spirit who gives us the inner assurance that it is indeed so, and our life of prayer, in which we call God "Abba, Father," as Jesus did, confirms that relationship.

> For you did not receive a spirit that makes you a slave again to fear, but you received the Spirit of sonship. And by him we cry, "Abba, Father." The Spirit himself testifies with our spirit that we are God's children. Now if we are children, then we are heirs—heirs of God and co-heirs with Christ, if indeed we share in his sufferings in order that we may also share in his glory. (Rom 8:15-17)

John, in his first letter, is very concerned to give his readers utter assurance of their salvation, and it is interesting that he weaves together, all the way through, both the objective facts of Jesus Christ and the subjective experience of God's love, love for other Christians, and the gift of the Holy Spirit. Here is a typical passage, but the whole epistle should be read in this light.

> We know that we live in him and he in us, because he has given us of his Spirit. And we have seen and testify that the Father has sent his Son to be the Savior of the world. If anyone acknowledges that Jesus is the Son of God, God lives in him and he in God. And so we know and rely on the love God has for us.
>
> God is love. Whoever lives in love lives in God, and God in him. (1 Jn 4:13-16)

And of course this makes it natural to add the fact that love is the primary fruit of the Holy Spirit (Gal 5:22-26). So another aspect of our assurance of salvation comes from the way our lives are being changed more and more into the image of Christ, through the work of the Holy Spirit. As we begin to bear the fruit of the Spirit, and to exercise the gifts of the spirit, and to "walk in the Spirit" (which means to live a changed life that is morally pleasing to God and a blessing to others), then we grow in our assurance of salvation because the evidence of that salvation at work within us is being seen in our lives.

QUESTIONS FOR REFLECTION OR DISCUSSION

1. Think of some local illustrations that make clear the difference between being saved *by* grace, while being saved through faith.

2. Is there a danger in your context that some evangelists and preachers make promises of salvation and all the blessings it involves, without regard for basing their teaching clearly on the Scriptures and the depth of the biblical story of salvation? What are the effects of such biblically deficient proclamation? How can you counteract it?

3. From reading this chapter, how would you help someone who says that they feel they can never really be sure about being saved?

6

Salvation and the Sovereignty of God

THE GREAT ACCLAMATION OF THE REDEEMED HUMANITY in Revelation has been occupying our thoughts all through this book. "Salvation belongs to our God," they cry, and we have explored many aspects of the resonance of those five words in biblical thinking. However, they do not stop there. "Salvation belongs to our God, *who sits on the throne,*" they continue.

And this is not surprising, of course, since the throne of God is the centerpiece of all the action in John's great vision in Revelation 4–7. What is at the center of the universe, perceived as a series of concentric circles of adoring humans, angels and creatures? A throne is. And who is on that throne? The Lord God Almighty. And what is he doing there? He is governing the whole of creation and history, all of which lies open to his gaze. This is the seat of cosmic government. This is the throne of God.

So salvation belongs to the God who governs all that exists in creation and all that happens in history. Salvation is the property of the God who is sovereign.

As we have seen already in abundance, it is the Old Testament Scriptures that provide so much of the background, imagery and vocabulary for the language and visions of the book of Revelation. Isaiah 6 and Ezekiel 1, for example, portray Yahweh seated on the throne, in a posture of awesome exaltation and authority. Both have probably influenced John's vision here.

So the song of *God's salvation* is also a song of *God's sovereignty*. What is the significance of this connection? At least four dimensions may be mentioned. The sovereignty of God in salvation must be taken into account in relation to our understanding of mission, the eschatological destiny of the nations, the destiny of the unevangelized and the extent of pastoral assurance.

GOD'S SOVEREIGNTY AND MISSION

The God who owns and rules the universe. One of the most astonishing affirmations about Yahweh the God of Israel is made in Deuteronomy 10:14-19. These six verses fall into two panels of three, with a matching pattern. The pattern is

- first, a hymn-like affirmation of a truth about Yahweh

- second, a surprising contrast

- third, a required response from God's people

It is helpful to set the two panels out side by side. See table 1.

Table 1. Deuteronomy 10:14-19

[14] To the LORD your God belong the heavens, even the highest heavens, the earth and everything in it.	[17] For the LORD your God is God of gods and Lord of lords, the great God, mighty and awesome, who shows no partiality and accepts no bribes.
[15] Yet the LORD set his affection on your forefathers and loved them, and he chose you, their descendants, above all the nations, as it is today.	[18] He defends the cause of the fatherless and the widow, and loves the alien, giving him food and clothing.
[16] Circumcise your hearts, therefore, and do not be stiff-necked any longer	[19] And you are to love those who are aliens, for you yourselves were aliens in Egypt

Deuteronomy 10:14 declares that Yahweh the God of Israel *owns* the universe. Deuteronomy 10:17 declares that Yahweh the God of Israel *rules* the universe. These are staggering claims, and each of them has enormous consequences in relation to mission. But before considering those consequences, it is important to notice first that these verses also speak about salvation. That is, they refer to God's love for Israel (Deut 10:15) and to God's redemption of Israel out of Egypt (Deut 10:19). However, God's redeeming love for Israel is set clearly within the context of God's sovereignty over all things. These rich verses combine in such a short space both the universality and the particularity of God. The God of the whole universe is the God who saved this people in particular. But equally, the God who loved and saved this people in particular, is the God who is sovereign over all universally.

This is the dual perspective that allows the redeemed to proclaim in Revelation 7:10 that *our* God sits *on the throne.* He has this particular saving relationship with *us,* his people. But he rules over *all.*

We must hold on to both poles of this biblical double affirmation. On the one hand, we must not emphasize the universal sovereignty of God in such a way as to dissolve the uniqueness and particularity of his saving action in and for Israel and his people in Christ. That would lead to a kind of universalism that is certainly not biblical: saying that everybody will be saved, no matter what they believe or do. But on the other hand, we must not emphasize the uniqueness of our saving relationship with "our God" in such a way as to capture God and limit him to our own ecclesiastical boundaries, as if he were not also the sovereign God of all nations, all history and all creation.

Salvation is God's property. God is not our property.

Turning now to the implications of those two staggering claims, let's think of the implications of God's cosmic ownership (Deut 10:14) and God's cosmic sovereignty (Deut 10:17).

God's cosmic ownership. Deuteronomy 10:14 makes the same enormous claim that we also find in Psalm 24:1 and Psalm 95:4-5. Everything in all creation belongs to the Lord God. There is nothing in creation that does not belong to him. There is nothing in the universe that belongs to any other so-called god.

This has *ethical* implications, for if the earth is the Lord's, it is not ours. The only sense in which it belongs to us is as God's tenants. He remains the divine landlord. He holds us responsible for how we use and manage it. There is thus an ecological dimension to the significance of this text. The earth is God's property; we need to be careful how we treat the property of the divine owner.

But there are also *missiological* implications, for this same affirmation is made about Jesus Christ. All creation belongs to Christ, as its creator, sustainer and heir (Col 1:15-18; Heb 1:2). That means that wherever we go in Christ's name, bearing good news of salvation, we are walking on his property. There is not an inch of the planet that does not already belong to Christ, by right. Whatever power or influence Satan and his demonic hosts exert over places or people is usurped, illegitimate, bogus and ultimately doomed. The universe belongs to the Lord—the Lord Jesus Christ.

God's cosmic sovereignty. Deuteronomy 10:17 complements Deuteronomy 10:14. It is not just that the Lord God created and therefore owns the whole universe; he is also the supreme authority over all powers and forces within creation—whether material or spiritual. Whatever they may be, Yahweh is Lord and God over all of them. He is the ruler of all that exists and governor of all that happens.

This too has missiological implications because the same claim is also made by and for Jesus in the New Testament. He calmly claimed that "all authority in heaven and earth has been given to me" (Mt 28:18). And Revelation takes the Old Testament language and applies it directly to the victory of Jesus: "the Lamb will overcome them because he is Lord of lords and King of kings" (Rev 17:14). Whatever other claims may be made in relation to other so-called lords and gods, says Paul, even if there are so-called gods, whether in heaven or on earth (as indeed there are many "gods" and many "lords"), yet for us there is but one God, the Father, from whom all things came and for whom we live; and there is but one Lord, Jesus Christ, through whom all things came and through whom we live. (1 Cor 8:5-6)

Such massive truth claims stand out against not only problems of meat and idols in ancient Corinth but also religious relativism and pluralism in our contemporary world.[1]

So as we bear witness to the salvation that God has accomplished for the world in Christ, we are fully authorized to do so. For the salvation we declare is the salvation that belongs to the God who sits on the throne. His is the name and authority that undergirds our message and our mission. Our mission flows from the cosmic lordship of Christ, whom the New Testament affirms to be in the same position as Yahweh—owner and ruler of the earth.

The God who calls all nations to salvation. Another text that may well have provided the specific reference for our verse in Revelation is Isaiah 40:22:

> He sits enthroned above the circle of the earth,
>   and its people are like grasshoppers.
> He stretches out the heavens like a canopy,
>   and spreads them out like a tent to live in.

Now when we are reading our text in Revelation 7, we have reached the end of the Bible's great story line. At that time—the climax of all history—the sovereignty of God will have been finally vindicated and will stand unchallenged. The whole universe will then acknowledge the rule of God through Christ. But back in the time of the book of Isaiah there is a very real contest going on.

Yahweh challenges all the gods of the nations—and especially the gods of Babylon—to appear in court, as it were, to see who has the right to claim to be truly God. Yahweh stakes his claim on the basis of his control over history. Only Yahweh had accurately declared history in advance and interpreted it in retrospect. Yahweh is, as he puts it, "the first and the last"—there before the beginning and there still at the end. There is no god other than him, no god before him or after him.

The result of this great contest is that the other gods and the nations who worship them are alike exposed as worthless failures and defeated rebels. Yahweh alone stands supreme. This is the overwhelming message of Isaiah 40–45.

But then a sudden and surprising message rings out. From the field of battle, from the judge's seat in the court, God calls out to those who are fleeing from his judgment,

> Gather together and come;
>> assemble, you fugitives from the nations.
> Ignorant are those who carry about idols of wood,
>> who pray to gods that cannot save.
> Declare what is to be, present it—
>> let them take counsel together.
> Who foretold this long ago,
>> who declared it from the distant past?
> Was it not I, the LORD?
>> And there is no God apart from me,
> a righteous God and a Savior;
>> there is none but me.
> Turn to me and be saved,
>> all you ends of the earth;
>> for I am God, and there is no other.
> By myself I have sworn,
>> my mouth has uttered in all integrity
>> a word that will not be revoked:
> Before me every knee will bow;
>> by me every tongue will swear.
> They will say of me, "In the LORD alone
>> are righteousness and strength." (Is 45:20-24)

This ringing invitation expresses the sovereignty of God in salvation, not just in judgment. It is not merely that Yahweh has dethroned the gods of the nations and announced their defeat. Yahweh now claims those nations and invites them to turn around toward him and be saved. They may think that their only option is to flee from God as their judge. But where can they flee? To whom can they turn? There is no other god. No other god that can save, anyway. So let them instead turn around (which of course is the biblical meaning of repentance), turn to the only living and saving God, and cast themselves on his saving righteousness and mercy:

- if Yahweh is sovereign over all the earth (which he is, for he created it)
- if Yahweh is the only source of salvation (which he is, for other gods cannot save)
- then Yahweh must be sovereign and savior for all nations, not just for Israel

This is the uniqueness and the universality of God combined into a single concept:

> There is no God apart from me,
> a righteous God and a Savior;
>   there is none but me. (Is 45:21)

This then is the affirmation that is made by the prophet, that Yahweh God is the only sovereign and savior to whom all people of all nations to the ends of the earth must turn if they are to be saved. And this likewise is the affirmation celebrated in Revelation by the redeemed humanity drawn from all nations, who can now speak of him as "our God," to whom all salvation and all sovereignty belong.

We, of course, live in between the anticipation of Isaiah 45 and the celebration of Revelation 7. Our task, therefore, is the missional one of taking the evangelistic appeal of God himself to people of all nations, inviting them to turn and be saved, so as to be among that great crowd who will sing this song. The missional task of God's people flows directly from the universal offer of salvation. And that in turn flows from the universal sovereignty of God—that is, from the very throne of God to the world.

This is also exactly the framework in which the Great Commission is set at the end of Matthew's Gospel. The risen Jesus speaks in terms that could only have been spoken by or in relation to God himself in the Old Testament, making the same claim as we read above from Deuteronomy 10:14 and 17. "All authority in heaven and on earth has been given to me," Jesus calmly affirmed. And on this foundation—the sovereign Lordship of Jesus Christ—the mission mandate follows immediately and inseparably, "so, as you go, disciple the nations" (Mt 28:18-19, my translation).

"Mission," as John Stott has said, "is an inescapable deduction from the Lordship of Christ."[2]

GOD'S SOVEREIGNTY AND THE DESTINY OF THE NATIONS

We have paid great attention to the *song* in Revelation 7, but who are the *singers?* Who does John hear celebrating that "salvation belongs to our God, who sits on the throne" (Rev 7:10)? It is "a great multitude that no one could count, from every nation, tribe, people and language" (Rev 7:9). The echo of the Abrahamic covenant could not be clearer. God is being called "our God," no longer just by Israelites, but by people drawn from "all nations"—just as God had promised Abraham.

The end of the Bible mirrors its beginning:

- The Bible begins with the story of creation, then moves on to the nations of humanity scattered in rebellion.

- The Bible ends with the nations of humanity gathered in praise, then moves on to a new creation.

What John witnesses in his great vision is the eschatological fulfillment of God's promise to Abraham. God had promised that Abraham's seed would be as uncountable as the stars or the sand and that people of all nations would be blessed through him. And God is faithful to his promises—a fact which is one more demonstration of his sovereignty. This is another reason why biblical salvation belongs to our God: it is our God who will have kept his promise. And in God's faithfulness to his own promises lies all hope of our salvation.

"All nations," God said to Abraham, who only just managed to believe it. After all, it was extremely unlikely that he and Sarah could have any children at all, let alone become a great nation through whom all nations would be blessed. But "all nations" was what God promised, so "all nations" it shall be.

It is surprising that the theme of the nations has not been given the prominence it deserves in biblical scholarship and writing. Yet it is unquestionably one of the major themes of the Bible. And God's plan for the nations of humanity is an integral part of the biblical doctrine of salvation. We can be so accustomed to thinking of salvation in purely individualistic terms that we neglect this fully biblical dimension of it. Likewise, the outworking of God's saving plan for the nations is a fundamental part of his sovereignty. Indeed, Paul links the two very clearly in Ephesians. There the plan of God is to bring all things together into a unity again in Christ—including all nations along with all creation. And this will happen according to the plan of the One who accomplishes all things according to the purpose of his will—that is to say, it is the focal point of God's exercised sovereignty.

It is too big a theme to tackle in depth here, but some summary is essential, in view of the fact that our control text specifically puts the song of salvation in the mouths of people of *all nations*. Where did Paul and John get their exalted vision of the destiny of the nations in God's saving plan? Where else but from the Scriptures they knew so well—the Old Testament.[3]

So as the Old Testament looked forward to God's plan of salvation for the nations, what did it include? Beyond the fulfillment of all God's predictions of the purging fires of judgment, what would salvation mean? For those who turn as "fugitives of the nations," as Isaiah called them, back to the living God, what did God promise to them? What, in other words, are the representatives of the nations whom John saw in his vision actually celebrating? Nothing less than the following incredible list of blessings (at least—and much more could be added). The nations will come to praise God because they will be

- registered in God's city
- blessed with God's salvation
- accepted in God's house
- called by God's name
- joined with God's people

Registered in God's city.

> Glorious things are said of you,
>   O city of God:
> "I will record Rahab and Babylon
>   among those who acknowledge me—
> Philistia too, and Tyre, along with Cush—
>   and will say, 'This one was born in Zion.'"
> Indeed, of Zion it will be said,
>   "This one and that one were born in her,
>   and the Most High himself will establish her."
> The LORD will write in the register of the peoples:
>   "This one was born in Zion." (Ps 87:3-6)

Psalm 87 uses the imagery of a register of the nations, and quite astonishingly holds the roll call in Zion itself. Many surrounding nations are listed as having been "born" there, and as being among those who "know me" (Ps 87:4 KJV, language normally exclusively used of Israel within the covenant relationship with Yahweh). The whole concept of

Zion is being redefined and extended. No longer a term or a place of exclusive privilege, Zion has here become an inclusive home for the nations. The expectation clearly is that Zion will ultimately come to include not just native-born Israelites but people of other nations who will be adopted and enfranchised as citizens of the city, with as much right as the native born to be registered there by God. The list of nations to be counted and registered as citizens of Zion even includes the two great historical *enemy* empires, Egypt (Rahab) and Babylon, along with smaller neighboring enemies, the Philistines, trading partners (Tyre) and representatives of the more distant regions (the black African kingdom of Cush).

When the roll is called up yonder, there will be some surprising names on the register. The way is being prepared for Revelation's picture of the city of God, into which the nations will bring their glory and wealth.

This psalm clearly anticipates New Testament teaching that believers in the Messiah Jesus have become as fully members of God's people as native-born Israelites ever were. You don't have to be born of Jewish ancestry to be a child of Abraham and a citizen of Zion. This turns into nonsense the efforts of some Christian groups to prove Jewish ancestry, as a kind of extra benefit.

In Peru, I was told by friends there, some Christians are being persuaded to pay money to an American agency that will explore their genealogy and provide them with documented proof that they have Jewish ancestors, and thus *really* belong to the Israel of God. This is not only shocking exploitation of gullible and untaught believers, but an even more shocking denial of the Bible's own teaching that such physical ancestry is of no importance at all as regards our salvation and inclusion in Christ and the people of God. Paul, who valued highly the heritage that he had as a Jew (the Scriptures, the covenants, the law, etc. [Rom 9:4-5]), vigorously repudiated the idea that his ethnic credentials were of any benefit at all in his salvation, and indeed counted them as "loss" in comparison to knowing the crucified and risen Messiah Jesus (Phil 3:2-11).

Blessed with God's salvation.

In that day there will be an altar to the LORD in the heart of Egypt, and a monument to the LORD at its border. It will be a sign and witness to the LORD Almighty in the land of Egypt. When they cry out to the LORD because of their oppressors, he will send them a savior and defender, and he will rescue them. So the LORD will make himself known to the Egyptians, and in that day they will acknowledge the LORD. They will worship with sacrifices and grain offerings; they will make vows to the LORD and keep them. The LORD will strike Egypt with a plague; he will strike them and heal them. They will turn to the LORD, and he will respond to their pleas and heal them.

In that day there will be a highway from Egypt to Assyria. The Assyrians will go to Egypt and the Egyptians to Assyria. The Egyptians and Assyrians will worship together. In that day Israel will be the third, along with Egypt and Assyria, a blessing on the earth. The LORD Almighty will bless them, saying, "Blessed be Egypt my people, Assyria my handiwork, and Israel my inheritance." (Is 19:19-25)

This breathtaking prophecy comes at the end of a chapter that has, in Isaiah 19:1-17, comprehensively placed Egypt under God's coming historical judgment, at every level of their religion, agriculture, fisheries, industry and politics. This is familiar stuff for prophets against the foreign nations of their own day.

But then, from Isaiah 19:18-22, the more indefinite eschatological future ("in that day") will see an astonishing transformation of Egypt's fortunes, in which they will experience for themselves all that God did for Israel when he rescued them from the Egyptian oppression. The prophet extends to a foreign nation promises of salvation in terms that are drawn from Israel's past (a new exodus, new covenant, new wilderness protection and land entry, etc.). Israel's past is used here to portray the future blessings of salvation that are now being promised to a *foreign* nation that turns to God. And not just any foreign nation, but the Egyptians—the archenemy of Israel in their great national epic. The Egyptians, who had once refused to acknowledge Yahweh, will cry out to him (not to their own gods). Yahweh will send them a *savior* and deliverer (as he had sent Moses). They will then know Yahweh and worship him (as Israel did through their exodus). They will be struck by plagues, but God will heal them. All this is Exodus revisited and turned inside out. This is Exodus reloaded, with the characters reversed.

As if what has been said about *Egypt* were not surprising enough, the prophet then brings *Assyria* into the equation and foretells that these two great nations would join hands (Is 19:23). Normally, the prospect of Egypt and Assyria in alliance would have filled Israelite hearts with dread. Egypt and Assyria were like giant nutcrackers, squeezing Israel at both ends of their biblical history and from opposite ends of the compass. But the purpose of their uniting will be not that they will join forces to fight *against* God and his people, but rather that "they will *worship* together."

The oppressors become worshipers. History is turned upside down in this vision of the future. The enemies of God and Israel will be at peace with Israel and with each other.

Now of course Isaiah speaks of Egypt and Assyria in a representational way; that is, they "stand for" a wider inclusion of other nations, not just the specifically named nations. This is often the way with Old Testament prophets. They spoke of the world of nations that they knew. And often (as in the first half of Is 19) they meant the actual nations that surrounded them in their own day. But when the prophets looked to the more distant future, some of these national names became representational, referring to great kingdoms or world empires in general, or to brutal political and military oppression in general, or to arrogant hostility toward God and his people in general. Thus, for example, it is clear that prophecies concerning *Babylon* (in both Old and New Testaments) move beyond predictions about the historical fate of the ancient city and empire of Babylon at the time of Nebuchadnezzar and become representational visions of other great world empires. Thus, for example, it is probable that Babylon in Revelation would have been understood as the Roman Empire by John's first readers, and has certainly been read as signifying other great oppressive world powers by later readers, and eventually speaks of the ultimate fate of the enemies of God. In the same way, Egypt and Assyria in the vision of Isaiah 19:19-25 represent people of all nations who will be brought by God from being enemies and threats to being among those who share in the blessing of salvation.

Then comes the final surprise: the identity of Israel will be *merged* with that of Egypt and Assyria. The prophet makes it unambiguous (not to mention scandalous) by applying to Egypt and Assyria descriptions that hitherto could only have been said about Israel. In fact, the word order in Hebrew is more emphatic and shocking than the translation in the New International Version. It reads (lit.): "Blessed be my people, Egypt(!), and the work of my hands, Assyria(!), and my inheritance, Israel." The shock of reading, "Egypt" immediately after "my people" (instead of the expected "Israel"), and of putting Israel third on the list, is palpable. Yet there it is. The archenemies of Israel will be absorbed into the identity, titles and privileges of Israel and share in the Abrahamic blessing of the living God, Yahweh. In fact they will become not only the beneficiaries of Abrahamic covenant (by being blessed), but will become agents of it benefiting others (by being a blessing in the earth).

Of course they will not be absorbed into God's people in this way while they remain enemies. The transformation that is explicit about Egypt must also be assumed about Assyria. It is only as God's enemies cry out to him, acknowledge him, worship him and turn to him (Is 19:20-22) that they enjoy rescue, healing, blessing and inclusion. Salvation is for those who turn to the living God in repentance and faith. That was just as true for rebellious Israel as for their traditional enemies.

But that indeed (bringing enemies to repentance and reconciliation) is what the converting love and power of God will accomplish—for the nations as for Israel. That is God's mission. God is in the business of turning enemies into friends, as Saul of Tarsus knew better than most. It is very possible that Paul's triple expression of the inclusion of the Gentiles within the identity and titles of Israel (as co-heirs, co-body and co-sharers with Israel) in Ephesians 3:6 owes something to Isaiah 19:25.

Accepted in God's house.

Let no foreigner who has bound himself to the LORD say,
    "The LORD will surely exclude me from his people."
And let not any eunuch complain,
    "I am only a dry tree."

For this is what the LORD says:
"To the eunuchs who keep my Sabbaths,
    who choose what pleases me
    and hold fast to my covenant—
to them I will give within my temple and its walls
    a memorial and a name
    better than sons and daughters;
I will give them an everlasting name
    that will not be cut off.
And foreigners who bind themselves to the LORD
    to serve him,
to love the name of the LORD,
    and to worship him,
all who keep the Sabbath without desecrating it
    and who hold fast to my covenant—
these I will bring to my holy mountain
    and give them joy in my house of prayer.
Their burnt offerings and sacrifices
    will be accepted on my altar;
for my house will be called
    a house of prayer for all nations." (Is 56:3-7)

These warm words were addressed not to nations as wholes, but to individual foreigners and eunuchs—two groups of people who feared that they would be excluded from God's people. Deuteronomy 23:1-8 said that castrated males (who could have no family) and certain categories of foreigners (who had no stake in the land) were indeed denied access to the holy assembly of Israelites at worship. But through the prophet, God transforms that deficit into something even greater. The eunuch will have "a memorial and a name" better than any family could give him. The foreigner will be brought to God's holy mountain—symbolic of having a rightful share in the land as a whole. They will, in short, be full citizens of Israel.

On what conditions were such promises made to foreigners? Precisely the same conditions that applied to Israel—namely, wholehearted covenant *loyalty* to Yahweh, exclusive *worship* of him and careful *obedience* to his laws (Is 56:4-6). *Anyone* who fulfilled those conditions would now be able to come right to the very heart of Israel's holy worship—God's altar in the temple. Nothing that was available to *Israelite* worshipers will be denied to *foreigners* who are willing to commit themselves to Israel's God. If they accept the terms of covenant membership, they will be accepted at the heart of the covenant relationship. They will find joy in the house of the LORD—the joy of identity and inclusion, the joy of salvation.

Once again, it is very probable that Paul's mind is saturated with the dynamic of these verses, as he wrote to Gentile believers who were benefiting from the fulfillment of them in Christ:

> Remember that at that time you [Gentiles] were separate from Christ, *excluded* from citizenship in Israel and foreigners to the covenants of the promise, without hope and without God in the world. But now in Christ Jesus you who were once far away have been *brought near* through the blood of Christ. (Eph 2:12-13, my italics)

And it is very probable that Luke had this passage of Isaiah in mind, with some ironic sense of humor no doubt, when he recorded that the first believer in Jesus from outside the ethnic Jewish community was in-

deed a *foreigner*, was a *eunuch* and was reading the scroll of *Isaiah*, just a
few column inches from this passage. Luke is careful to point out, however, that even though the Ethiopian eunuch in Acts 8 had indeed been
to Jerusalem to worship, he found *joy* (as the prophet promised), not in
the *temple* but when he heard about *Jesus*, trusted and was baptized, and
went on his way rejoicing. *Jesus* is the one through whom people of all
nations will be accepted in God's house of prayer for all nations. For
Jesus himself is that new and living temple.

   Called by God's name.

> "In that day I will restore
>   David's fallen tent.
> I will repair its broken places,
>   restore its ruins,
>   and build it as it used to be,
> so that they may possess the remnant of Edom
>   and all the nations that bear my name,"
> declares the LORD, who will do these things. (Amos 9:11-12)

These verses bring the book of Amos to a startling close. After the fires
of judgment, destruction and exile that have dominated the whole book
so far, the final note is one of hope. Beyond judgment lies restoration.
What is also striking is that, just as Amos began in the international
arena, so he ends there. Amos 1—2 declares God's anger against the cha-
otic wickedness of the surrounding nations (and both Judah and Israel
are no better). These final verses in the closing chapter portray the restoration not only of the Davidic kingdom and temple but also of "the
remnant of Edom and *all the nations that bear my name.*"

   The great surprise here is the combination of a plural word, *nations*,
with the concept "called by my name." Only one nation, surely, could be
legitimately described in that way. The expression "called by the name
of" denotes ownership and intimate relationship. Being called by Yahweh's name applied to the central focal points of Israel's unique relation-

ship with Yahweh. The *ark of the covenant* was called by his name (2 Sam 6:2). So was the *temple* itself, on the day of its dedication, and Solomon prayed that "all the peoples of the earth" would come to know it (1 Kings 8:43). *Jerusalem*, worthily or not, was the city that was called by Yahweh's name (Jer 25:29). Most significant of all, it was at the heart of God's covenant blessing on Israel that they would be the *people* who were called by his name.

> The LORD will establish you as his holy people, as he promised you on oath, if you keep the commands of the LORD your God and walk in his ways. Then all the peoples on earth will see that you are *called by the name* of the LORD, and they will fear you. (Deut 28:9-10, my italics)

Indeed, this was precisely one of the distinguishing marks of Israel, for the foreign nations of Israel's own day could be lumped together simply as those had *never* been called by Yahweh's name (Is 63:19).

So what is Amos saying, then? In his day, it was the defining privilege of *only one people on earth*—Israel—to be known as the nation "called by the name of Yahweh." But eventually, declares the prophet, this identity will be available to people of "all the nations." How much more included could you get? The nations who had stood under God's judgment along with Israel in Amos 1—2 now stand under God's blessing along with Israel in these closing verses. The very concept of Israel has been stretched to include the nations in the key designation, "called by my name."

Joined with God's people.

> "Shout and be glad, O Daughter of Zion. For look, here I am coming, and I will reside in the midst of you," declares the LORD. "Many nations will join themselves to Yahweh in that day. And they will be for me for a people. And I will reside in the midst of you." (Zech 2:10-11, my translation)

These verses come in the midst of a vision of encouragement to the postexilic people of Jerusalem. In contrast to the program initiated by Nehemiah, Zechariah says that the city of God will not need walls, partly because its influx of new inhabitants will be so many, and partly because God himself will be a wall of fire around them (Zech 2:3-5). Their enemies who had plundered them will themselves be defeated and plundered (Zech 2:8-9). Then the King will come home to dwell once more among his people.

So the prophet's message for Israel was not one of exclusive favoritism at the hand of God, but of an *expansion* that would include not only their own returning exiles but also people of "many nations." And the prophet's message for the nations was not one of destructive judgment only but, beyond that, of inclusion in God's people. And notice how total is that inclusion.

First, the nations will join themselves *to Yahweh*—not merely to Israel. In other words, the nations do not join God's people merely as subordinates of Israel, in some second-class citizenship. No, they will belong to Yahweh just as much as Old Testament Israel did.

Second, the nations will enjoy exactly the same covenantal relationship with Yahweh that Israel did. The expression "they will be for me for a people" is precisely the language of the covenant, with its roots going back to Sinai. It is a relationship only ever applied to Israel before. Significantly, although the nations are plural (as is the verb "they will be"), the predicate is singular—"*a people.*" This is not Israel *plus* the nations, but the nations *as* Israel—one people belonging to God.

Zion will become a multinational community of people from many nations, all of whom will belong to Yahweh, and therefore be rightly counted as belonging to Israel. God himself will dwell in the midst of "you"—Zion of the nations (cf. Ps 87). The identity and membership of Israel have thus been radically redrawn by Yahweh himself. It is no longer Zion *and* the nations, but Zion *inclusive of* the nations. It is not that God will *replace* Israel and Zion with some new religion (Christianity?), but rather that Israel and Zion will expand to include people of all nations, in a redefined and extended covenant people of God—the multinational community of believers in Christ.

These are the kind of Old Testament texts that feed the New Testament understanding of God's plan of salvation for the nations. Paul was convinced that this great vision was now coming to fulfillment with the arrival of the Messiah, Jesus. His death and resurrection opened the door for people of any nation and all nations to be saved and join the community of God's redeemed, covenant people. This was the gospel he preached to the Gentiles. The book of Acts showed how they responded eagerly to such good news. The book of Revelation shows how the grand total of all those from every nation who will have so responded will one day gather as the redeemed humanity in the new creation to praise the God, through whose sovereignty this great salvation has been offered to all nations.

GOD'S SOVEREIGNTY AND THE EXTENT OF SALVATION

This is the context in which it is appropriate to think about another issue that many find disturbing: the question of whether and how any persons may be saved who are, from our point of view, unevangelized. As we approach that topic, we must keep in mind all we have just been considering about God's gracious sovereignty over all nations, and the biblical affirmations that God's saving purpose is to include people from all nations among the redeemed who will inhabit the new creation and sing the song of salvation to our God and to the Lamb.

Ancestors who never heard the gospel. I have stressed throughout this book that salvation is a matter of what God has done. Biblical salvation is constituted by the story of those great saving acts of God, centered of course on the death and resurrection of Jesus Christ. And in chapter five I pointed out that people come into the experience of salvation through hearing that story and putting their faith in the Christ who stands at the center of it.

But what about those who never hear the story? "Salvation belongs to our God . . . and to the Lamb." But what if people never hear about "our God," or about the "Lamb who was slain"? That is, they never hear of the

God of the Bible, or about Jesus of Nazareth and his life, death and resurrection? What if they lived and died in ages past before the news of the
gospel story could ever have reached them—ages before Christ, or even
before Abraham? What if they live now in some part of the world where
the gospel story has never yet been heard—and die before it is ever told?
Is there any hope that *any* such people—the unevangelized, in other
words—will ever, or could ever, experience the blessing of God's salvation? Or is there categorically no hope that such a thing is even possible?

This is an urgent and sometimes distressing question to those who are
among the first generation to come to faith in Christ for themselves
within a culture where family bonds are strong and stretch back through
past generations of ancestors. This is a common phenomenon in new
churches planted by Christian mission efforts in parts of Asia and Africa
especially. Evangelists are faced with anguished questions: What about
my parents, grandparents or great grandparents—all of whom died before you came to tell us this message about Jesus? They did not know
about Jesus. Do you mean that they have all gone to hell? Is there no
hope that any of them could have been saved by God? If I become a believer, am I cut off from my family (living and dead) forever?

I said these are pressing questions in Africa and Asia, but that is because so many cultures there have preserved their strong sense of family
identity and belonging. For those of us who live in Western cultures, it
is only to our shame that such questions are not more pressing than they
ought to be. The acids of individualism have so eroded our sense of kinship identity that we scarcely know our grandparents, let alone any ancestors further back, and the question of whether people many
generations back in our genealogical tree were Christian believers hardly
crosses our minds, let alone causes us grief and anxiety. So long as I'm
saved, and if possible my immediate living family, not much before that
seems to worry us.

And I said that it is a pressing question for first-generation believers,
whose recent ancestors died before the gospel ever reached them, bring-

ing the possibility of conscious, articulate faith in Jesus. For Christians in countries where there has been a Christian presence for centuries, of course, the problem is not quite the same—our ancestors (for centuries back at least) did have an *opportunity* of hearing and responding to the gospel, whether they took it or not. And yet, this is only a relative comparison. After all, even those of us born in Britain, for example, if we are truly indigenous natives of those islands, have ancestors that once lived and died before the gospel ever reached them. Those ancestors may have lived two thousand years ago, but what is that in God's sight, or the great sweep of history? A thousand years are as one day with God. Whether African, Asian, European, American (North or South), Aboriginals, Islanders or whatever else, we are all, in principle, in the same boat. We *all* have ancestors who lived and died among the unevangelized, without the knowledge of the gospel. Has God saved any of them? Is there any hope of such a possibility?

Salvation—*only through Christ, or only through knowledge of Christ?* One of the core beliefs of biblical Christianity is that salvation is through Jesus Christ alone. There is no salvation other than in and through Jesus. We have argued this biblically throughout this book. Salvation is available to human beings only because of what God has done in and through his Son, the Lord Jesus Christ—from no other source and on no other foundation.

The question that is asked, however, is this: Does that necessarily mean that salvation is only available through actual *knowledge* of Jesus Christ and conscious faith in him?[4] We fully accept and affirm that all those who will finally be saved and will join the redeemed people of God in the new creation will, without exception, be saved on the sole basis of the cross of Christ. All salvation is because of what God has done in and through Jesus Christ, his incarnate Son. All who will be saved will be saved because Jesus died for them. Whoever God saves, he saves for Jesus' sake. There is no other source, or basis, or means of salvation. So whoever we meet in the new creation will be there for the same reason we will be: because Jesus died for them and God saved them through the atoning blood of Christ.

But is it possible for anyone to be saved by Christ and because of Christ's death who has not heard of Christ and thus cannot explicitly exercise trust in him as a known name and person?

This question is sometimes framed in theological language: Even if one grants the *ontological* necessity of Christ for salvation (no other means of salvation exists), is there also an *epistemological* necessity (you have to *know* about Christ in order to be saved by him)? We must think very clearly about the question itself before trying to answer it.

We are *not* asking if people can be saved by some other way than by Christ, such as by another religion; that is not at issue, because the Bible makes it clear that there is no salvation outside of the work of Christ.

We are *not* asking whether people who reject Christ might nevertheless possibly be saved (as in some forms of universalism). Rather, the question refers only to those who have had no opportunity in their lifetimes to hear about him and make any kind of choice regarding him— those who have never heard the gospel, the unevangelized. Is there any possibility that God saves any from among such people, saving them through Christ even though they have not heard of him? That is the question. Can or will any of the unevangelized be saved?

Among Christians who would equally claim to believe the Bible and accept its authority, there are mainly two different answers given to this question. There are those who answer with an emphatic negative. There is simply no possibility of any of the unevangelized being saved. They are, by definition, ignorant of the gospel and therefore, by definition, eternally lost. There are others who answer with cautious optimism. They believe that the Bible itself gives us grounds to hope that God, in his mercy and for Christ's sake, will have saved some (or many; there are different views on this) from among unevangelized peoples.

No hope of salvation for any among the unevangelized. All human beings stand under the just judgment of God for their sin and rebellion.

The only way of salvation is through repentance and faith in the saving work of Christ on the cross. Therefore, those who never hear of Jesus in their lives on this earth are eternally lost. This is sometimes supported by the argument that if this were not so, what motive would be left for evangelism?[5] The biblical basis for such a view of the matter is strongly built on texts that undoubtedly teach that Jesus is the only way to God and to salvation.

> I am the way and the truth and the life. No one comes to the Father except through me. (Jn 14:6)

> Salvation is found in no one else [than Jesus], for there is no other name under heaven given to men by which we must be saved. (Acts 4:12)

> "Everyone who calls on the name of the Lord will be saved."
> How, then, can they call on the one they have not believed in? And how can they believe in the one of whom they have not heard? And how can they hear without someone preaching to them? And how can they preach unless they are sent? As it is written, "How beautiful are the feet of those who bring good news!"
> But not all the Israelites accepted the good news. For Isaiah says, "Lord, who has believed our message?" Consequently, faith comes from hearing the message, and the message is heard through the word of Christ. (Rom 10:13-17)[6]

This view clearly defines and defends the uniqueness of Christ for salvation in unequivocal terms. Not only is Christ himself the only means of salvation available to humanity, but, also, hearing and responding to the gospel of Christ is the only means by which the salvation achieved by Christ can be received. The unevangelized simply *cannot* be saved, for they lack the only means by which they could be— i.e., knowledge of the gospel.

Now such a view has many opponents, of course. But some of those who object to it are guilty of distorting it, and then attacking the caricature, not the argument itself. One particular distortion is commonly put forward. "How can you believe that God will condemn people to hell just because they have not believed in Jesus, if they have never heard of him? It is not their fault that they have not heard of Jesus, since they have never been evangelized, so it is manifestly unfair to condemn them for not responding to the gospel." This point of view can be made to sound so plausible and apparently convincing that it is especially important to think very carefully and clearly at this point.

The Bible never teaches that God condemns people because they have not responded to the Christ of whom they have never heard. What the Bible does unquestionably and uncompromisingly teach is that *all* human beings are sinful and stand rightly and justly under God's judgment, whether they have heard of Christ or not. Condemnation is based on our sinful actions, not on our ignorance.

Of course the Bible also shows clearly that not everybody is as wicked as everybody else; and that not everybody is as wicked as they could be. But the Bible leaves us in no doubt of the fundamental and universal fact of human sinfulness and wickedness. "All have sinned and fall short of the glory of God," says Paul (Rom 3:23), among many other Bible writers. And it is this universal fact of human sin that is the reason for God's judgment. Those who will finally experience the wrath of God and all that is intended by the Bible's warnings about hell will do so *not* because of what they did *not* know and therefore *could not* do (i.e., trust in Jesus) but because of all they *did* know and nevertheless *did do,* in spite of all they knew. All people sin against the light of conscience and the knowledge of God that is available to all human beings. Our sin lies in what we do in the wake of what we know (we sin in spite of the knowledge of God)—not in what we do not do because we did not know (failure to trust in Jesus because of never having heard of him).

> The wrath of God is being revealed from heaven against all the godlessness and wickedness of men who suppress the truth by their wickedness, since what may be known about God is plain to them, because God has made it

plain to them. For since the creation of the world God's invisible qualities—his eternal power and divine nature—have been clearly seen, being understood from what has been made, so that men are without excuse.

For although they knew God, they neither glorified him as God nor gave thanks to him, but their thinking became futile and their foolish hearts were darkened. (Rom 1:18-21)

To put it more bluntly and simply: nobody will go to hell simply because they never heard of Jesus; they will go to hell because of their sin and rebellion in the sight of God, which the Bible affirms is the universal, default, condition of all humanity. The basis of our condemnation is not our ignorance but our deliberate sin.

People are unevangelized through no fault of their own. True. But nobody will suffer the wrath of God through no fault of their own. God's judgment will be clearly and unequivocally just and deserved.

Hope of salvation for some among the unevangelized. There are other Christians who would just as strongly affirm that the cross of Christ is the only basis for human salvation, but who would be less certain that the number of the saved will ultimately be limited to those who hear the gospel and consciously trust in Jesus Christ. They wish to leave open the possibility (and some would hold it as an affirmation) that God will save *through Christ* some who, even though they never hear about Christ in their earthly lifetimes, nevertheless turn to God in some kind of repentance and faith. Only God can evaluate such turning with his intimate knowledge of every human heart. But wherever anyone seeks God in that way, it is a result of the grace of God at work in human hearts and lives, and, according to Paul, it happens because God desires it.

From one ancestor he made all nations to inhabit the whole earth, and he allotted the times of their existence and the boundaries of the places where they would live, so that they would search for God and perhaps grope for him and find him—though indeed he is not far from each one of us. (Acts 17:26-27 NRSV)

Several arguments are put forward in support of this view.

Old Testament believers. There were believers in the Old Testament whom we would unquestionably regard as saved, yet they never knew about the historical Jesus of Nazareth. Their salvation was still a matter of God's grace and initiative, and it was based on the sacrifice of Christ, yet to come in history. That is, they were indeed saved *by* Christ (whose death is effective for all human history), but not through *knowing* Christ (in the sense of knowing the story of the life, death and resurrection of Jesus of Nazareth—the New Testament gospel).

Now of course we could not exactly call the people of Israel in the Old Testament "unevangelized." They certainly did have their unique revelation of God as Yahweh with all the redemptive and covenantal depths that flowed through their historical experience of God. They received the good news of God's historical redemption, in the exodus, and his promises of salvation through their Messiah king in the future. We have seen in this book that the Old Testament Israelites had a very broad and deep understanding of salvation and of the God of their salvation.

Nevertheless, the fact remains that Old Testament Israelites did not know the historical Jesus of Nazareth. They did not hear the preaching of the cross of Christ and the necessity of repentance and faith in him. They were not evangelized in a New Testament sense, with the gospel we read in the Gospels, Acts and the Epistles. They believed in God in response to what they knew of God through the progress of Old Testament revelation to that point. And to those who sought to turn toward God in humble repentance, faith and obedience (like the psalmists), God responded in grace and saving righteousness.

Abraham is the model of this saving faith, expressed through obedience, in both testaments. "Abraham believed the LORD, and he credited it to him as righteousness" (Gen 15:6; cf. Rom 4:3). According to Paul, Abraham did respond to the gospel, but not the gospel in its New Testament form as related specifically to Jesus Christ. Rather, Paul says, "the Scripture . . . announced *the gospel in advance* to Abraham: 'All nations will be blessed through you'" (Gal 3:8, my italics). The good news in the context of Genesis was that God intended to bless all the nations of humanity in spite of sin and rebellion and to do so by means of the descendants of Abraham. This is what Abraham believed, and his faith in God's promise was counted as saving righteousness.

Non-Israelite believers. We may agree that the Israelite believers stood in a special position. But the Old Testament also describes how God responded graciously to others who did *not* stand within the covenant nation, such as "converts" like Rahab (Josh 2), Ruth (Ruth 1:16-17), the widow of Zarephath (1 Kings 17:24) and Naaman (2 Kings 5:15-18), and repentant sinners such as the Ninevites (Jonah). All of these joined the community of the saved by coming to exercise faith in the God they encountered through the testimony of Israelites—so in a sense they could be called "evangelized"—even if it was nothing like the New Testament gospel that they heard. They are individual examples of the great Old Testament vision of people from all nations being blessed through the people of Abraham.

But then there were also those who were saved who lived long before the redemptive revelation embodied in the history of Israel had even begun—i.e., before Abraham—such as Enoch. This may also include some proverbially righteous people like Noah, Job and Daniel (Ezek 14:14, 20). Such people were not only living B.C. (before Christ), but also B.A. (before Abraham).

Enoch's faith is held up also in the New Testament as a model. His was the kind of faith which is required in order to please God.

> [Enoch] was commended as one who pleased God. And without faith it is impossible to please God, because anyone who comes to him must *believe that he exists* and that he rewards those who *earnestly seek him.* (Heb 11:5-6, my italics)

Obviously the writer of Hebrews could not speak about faith *in Jesus* since that was impossible for Enoch. However, Enoch certainly trusted

God and earnestly sought him, and God saved him and took him to himself. So the question can be asked: Have there been and are there still other people who fulfill the conditions of Enoch—that is, who believe God exists and earnestly seek him? And if so, does not God save them in the same way, for the same reason (their faith) and on the same basis— the death of Christ?

If, then, the Bible itself tells us that it was possible for people in those ages before Christ to be saved by Christ without actually knowing Christ, because it was *historically* impossible for them to do so, is it not similarly possible for people today to be saved by Christ even if they do not know him because of *geographical* and other obstacles? Such people are living chronologically A.D. But in fact they are as yet informationally B.C. That is to say, in terms of their knowledge, they are in the same position as those who lived before Christ. Are there people like Enoch among them, who believe in God and earnestly seek him? Those who hold this position want to hope so and to believe that if there are, then God responds to them in saving grace. But only God knows who, or how many, they are. For only God knows the hearts of every individual.

A great multitude that no one could count. Our control text tells us that the song of salvation will be sung by "a great multitude that no one could count, from *every* nation, tribe, people and language" (Rev 7:9, my italics). This is very similar to the affirmation of the Old Testament in places like Psalm 86:

> *All the nations* you have made
>> will come and worship before you, O Lord;
>> they will bring glory to your name. (Ps 86:9, my italics)

Now such language could be taken in a general or approximate sense. That is, it could mean only that there will be all kinds of people from all kinds of ethnic backgrounds who will be saved and bring their worship to God. But if we take it in a more intentional sense, then it is affirming that God will have saved people from *every* ethnic, cultural and linguistic group in the human race throughout history.

Now if that is what Revelation 7:9 (along with Ps 86:9) intends to say, then the final number of the redeemed will certainly include more than those who have been explicitly evangelized by Christian missionaries in the centuries after Pentecost. For many tribes and peoples and languages have died out in human history long before the gospel could ever have reached them. Indeed many peoples and languages died out long before Christ was even born, in the great swaths of human culture in the millennia B.C. So if, on the Last Day, some people will have been saved from among such tribes and peoples, then they will have been saved by Christ, but without having heard of Christ.

Now, if we want to argue along this line, we have to be very careful to understand what is being said, and what is *not* being said.

First, this is not universalism, which believes that everybody will be saved no matter what they believe or how they live. That kind of universalism is clearly contradicted by the Bible. Rather, this view is saying that there is a basic principle that applies to all human beings, namely, that we are saved by God's grace only, received through the channels of repentance and trust in God's mercy. If any human being, realizing his or her own inability to live even by the standards of personal conscience, repents of self-effort and failure, and turns to plead the mercy of God, however he or she envisages God, will God not respond in the saving grace of Christ, even if the person never hears of Christ in this life?

Second, this view is not saying that good and sincere people in any other faith, or within Christianity either, are saved by their goodness and sincerity. In fact it is the precise opposite of that. In Jesus' shocking parable of the tax collector and the Pharisee, it was the religious man in his very commendable goodness who was not justified, while the sinner who could do nothing but cry for mercy went home, according to Jesus, "justified before God" (Lk 18:14). All who will be saved in the end will be saved by the grace of God, not because of goodness or merit. The heart of the gospel is that God saves sinners who know they are sinners and turn away from sin and self toward God.

Third, this view is not saying that people in other faiths can be saved through the sacraments of their own religious systems, or that other religions are provisional ways of salvation. The New Testament does not talk of salvation at all except in and through Christ. In any case, as was made very clear earlier, it is God who saves, not religions. It is one thing to believe that God may save through the sacrifice of Christ a person who turns toward God in repentance and faith within the context of another religion (simply because that is where he or she happens to live). It is quite different to say the person is saved by means of another religion. Even if we accept the possibility of the first, we are not thereby affirming the second.

Sovereign grace. Speaking for myself, I find myself unable to accept that the first position above is an adequate account of what the Bible as a whole teaches. We have seen that the whole emphasis of the Bible lies on salvation being something that God has accomplished in history and that belongs to God in his sovereignty. It seems to me to be presumptuous for us to limit the sovereignty of God's saving grace to the evangelistic obedience of the church (or more often, the lack of it). That is to say, while I strongly affirm that people can only be saved by Christ, and that the normal way that God brings salvation is through those who know Christ witnessing to those who do not yet and leading them to repentance and faith (i.e., evangelism), I cannot take the further step of saying that God is somehow unable or unwilling to save anybody at any time in human history, unless and until a Christian reaches them with an intelligible explanation of the story of the gospel.

Such a view, if pressed to its theological limits, would mean that in the end, the elect of God (that is, those who will constitute the final number of the redeemed inhabitants of the new creation) will be a subset of those evangelized by us. It would be saying: only those who have been evangelized can be saved, but not all who are evangelized actually are saved; so the total number saved (by God) will be smaller than the

total number evangelized (by us). And that seems to restrict the operation of God's grace to the limits of the operation of our human evangelistic efforts.

It seems to me that the Bible gives us grounds to believe that the reverse will be true. That is, those who will have responded to explicit
Christian evangelism will be a subset of the finally elect and redeemed.
For God operates in his sovereign grace to reach out to and touch people
to the ends of the earth and at all times of history. The history of Christian mission has many examples of encounters with people who had had
an experience of, or some revelation of, the saving grace of God even before Christian missionaries arrived, and who therefore welcomed the
news about Jesus with open arms. What the Old Testament prepares us
to expect—namely the appearance of God-fearing people in the most
unlikely places (even among the enemies of God's people)—is replicated
in the history of crosscultural mission.

No reduction of evangelistic motivation. The hopeful possibility that
God may in his sovereign grace save some whom the church may never
reach with the gospel (or who died before the church could ever have
reached them) does not in any way lessen the church's obligation in mission and evangelism. We know that the human race universally lives in
a state of sin and stands under God's judgment. All have sinned. All are
eternally lost, apart from the saving grace of God. We know that God has
provided the means of salvation in the cross and resurrection of Christ.
We know that we are commanded by Christ himself to make these facts
known to the nations and to call men and women everywhere to respond to them in repentance, faith and obedience. We have no liberty to
preach otherwise if we are to be obedient to this commission.

If, however, God in the sovereignty of his grace, but independent
of human evangelistic activity, initiates in the heart of any human being
a response of repentance and faith which leads to final salvation
through Christ, then, unless we meet such a person later in this life, this
act of faith and salvation will by definition be unknown to us and

known only to God. It will be a matter of rejoicing and giving greater glory to God when we do meet them, here or in the new creation. But it gives us no more valid reason to disobey the Great Commission than does the biblical doctrine of election, though that too has been accused of being a disincentive to evangelism. For in the end, the only way we can be sure, from our own observational perspective, that people are being saved is as we are faithful in our witness and see people responding in repentance and faith to Christ. That is our task and our joy. Beyond that, let God be God.

Let God be God. By this I mean that, after all our discussion of the arguments above, it may well be a wiser and humbler approach to say that the very question itself is not one we should be asking, or expecting a simple answer to. Part of the implication of affirming that "salvation belongs to our God" is to allow him to choose whom he saves. Deuteronomy 29:29 reminds us that there are secret things that belong to the Lord alone. Paul reminds us that "the Lord knows those who are his" (2 Tim 2:19).

- We know that all human beings *need* to be saved, for we are otherwise dead in our sins and under condemnation for our wickedness.

- We know that God sent his Son into the world to save sinners.

- We know that God longs to bring people to salvation, for "I take no pleasure in the death of the wicked, but rather that they turn from their ways and live" (Ezek 33:11).

- We know that God has provided the way of salvation, through the blood of Christ, shed on the cross for our forgiveness.

- We know that those who put their faith in Christ can be assured of their salvation. But we should not stray into dictating to God the limits of salvation, or claiming that we know for certain what the eternal destiny of those who have died actually is, for only God is their Judge.

I was horrified shortly after the terrible tsunami of December 26,

2004, to hear a Christian preacher speak dogmatically about "hundreds of thousands of people who went straight to hell." Who gave him the right to affirm such a thing? They went straight into the presence of the God who is their creator and judge, the God of perfect justice and mercy, of holy wrath and holy love, the God who knows the sin of the sinner, the pain of the sinned against and the secrets of every human heart. Only this God determines the eternal destiny of every human being.

And this, it seems to me, is the way to handle those questions about ancestors who died before the arrival of Christian evangelists. It seems to me as wrong to say with adamant certainty that they have all undoubtedly gone to hell as it is equally wrong to say with misguided compassion that they have all gone to heaven. What we can say with clear biblical warrant is that they have gone into the hands of the God who made them, loved them, sent Christ to die for them and knows everything they ever did or did not do, and everything they did or did not know—and will judge them with perfect justice and mercy. We may be ashamed that the gospel did not reach these new believers until so late. But we may be equally sure that God loved their ancestors no less than he loves the descendants, and that "the Judge of all the earth [will] do right" (Gen 18:25).

GOD'S SOVEREIGNTY AND PASTORAL ASSURANCE

This leads us back to the question of pastoral assurance in relation to salvation in all its dimensions. In chapter one we surveyed the great variety of ways in which the Bible uses the language of salvation. In the Bible narratives God saves people in many different ways. And all salvation "belongs to our God, who sits on the throne" (Rev 7:10). That means, then, that *all* the dimensions of biblical salvation still remain within the sovereign disposal of God. God still has the power to heal people from sickness, to rescue from danger, deliver from death, release from oppression, forgive sin, pardon guilt and grant the supreme gift of God—eternal life in the age to come, the new creation. Any and all of these outworkings of God's saving power are still within God's sovereign gift. Pastorally, however, they are not all on the same level of assurance.

What is guaranteed? As we engage in evangelistic or pastoral ministry, what exactly can we promise to those who turn to God in repentance and faith? We have every scriptural foundation for affirming to sinners that if they repent and trust in the saving work of Christ they can know the forgiveness of sins, they can be assured of salvation from God's wrath on the last day, and they can be sure they have received the gift of eternal life. As we saw in chapter five, the assurance of eternal salvation rests on the explicit and abundant promises of God in the Bible. We can know for certain that when we turn from sin and put our faith in Jesus Christ, God freely and fully pardons our sin (forgiveness), puts us into a right relationship with himself (justification), gives us new life (regeneration), removes the enmity between us (reconciliation) and brings us into his family (adoption). In other words, the promises of God guarantee that, *in relation to sin and its eternal consequences,* we have been saved, we are being saved, and we will be saved, and all on the basis of the cross and resurrection of Jesus Christ. These are the great truths of biblical salvation that we can confidently trust for ourselves and promise to others on the basis of God's own explicit promises.

But what about the many other things that the Bible speaks of in saving language—healing, liberation from oppression, rescuing from danger and death, etc? These are all things that happen in this life. And the Bible shows that God can and often does work to make them true for some people in particular times and places. But is it a biblical promise that he always will do so, all the time, for everyone who asks or trusts? Does faith *guarantee* delivery of all the other dimensions of God's saving power *in this life?*

There are some kinds of Christian preaching and teaching that appear to claim just this. Some forms of prosperity teaching claim that it is *always* God's will to save you from poverty and make you rich—here and now. Some healing campaigns claim that it is *always* God's will to save you from sickness and make you well—here and now. Faith, it is said, is the key. Have faith, or enough faith, or the right kind of faith, and all the benefits of God's salvation can be yours in this present life. You don't need to wait to get to heaven.

So does faith guarantee every kind of salvation we can think of, including those that the Bible uses the vocabulary of salvation for? Not according to Hebrews 11.

Faith and salvation in Hebrews 11. In Hebrews 11 we have a catalog of the saving acts of God in relation to the faith of many individuals in the Old Testament. Some are named, some are anonymous, but the one thing they all had in common was faith. Now according to Hebrews 11:32-35, many of them experienced material, physical and military dimensions of God's salvation, even though they did not yet finally experience all that God had promised them (any more than we have, yet).

> And what more shall I say? I do not have time to tell about Gideon, Barak, Samson, Jephthah, David, Samuel and the prophets, who through faith conquered kingdoms, administered justice, and gained what was promised; who shut the mouths of lions, quenched the fury of the flames, and escaped the edge of the sword; whose weakness was turned to strength; and who became powerful in battle and routed foreign armies. Women received back their dead, raised to life again. (Heb 11:32-35)

But in a highly significant turn in Hebrews 11:35, *others did not* experience salvation in this immediate way.

> *Others* were tortured and refused to be released, so that they might gain a better resurrection. Some faced jeers and flogging, while still others were chained and put in prison. They were stoned; they were sawed in two; they were put to death by the sword. They went about in sheepskins and goatskins, destitute, persecuted and mistreated—the world was not worthy of them. They wandered in deserts and mountains, and in caves and holes in the ground. (Heb 11:35-38, my italics)

So then, the writer tells us, there were those who, even though they exercised faith just as much as those in the first list, were tortured to death but were not delivered. They were attacked but never received earthly vindication. They were imprisoned without release, oppressed without justice, impoverished without relief. Salvation in those senses never came for them, in their earthly lifetimes.

For every Shadrach, Meshach and Abednego, who were delivered because they knew that "the God we serve *is able to save* us" (Dan 3:17, my italics), there have been many others who perished amidst the flames or the lions. For such people, what Daniel's three friends allowed as a possibility—"but even if he does not" (Dan 3:18)—became the reality. In some situations, without explanation, God chooses *not* to save people from such evils.

But, the writer to the Hebrews goes on, "these were *all* commended for their faith," even though their salvation did not materialize in their earthly circumstances.

> *These were all commended for their faith,* yet none of them received what had been promised. God had planned something better for us so that only together with us would they be made perfect. (Heb 11:39-40, my italics)

This passage should be written up against all false and exaggerated claims for instant health and wealth as the inevitable product of faith. Some *were* saved (in the earthly sense), others were *not*—but they all had faith and were commended for it. The difference, then, lay not in the presence or absence of faith but in the mysterious ways of God. God remains sovereign. Salvation, in all its senses, belongs to God. We can promise what God unquestionably promises (eternal salvation for those who repent and trust him). But we should not promise what God does not promise (deliverance from all problems or suffering in this life).

Eternity and history. So then, we have to recognize that, according to the Bible, it is possible to be saved from sin for all *eternity* and yet not be delivered from danger, disease or death in *history.* Two bandits were crucified beside Jesus. Neither of them was saved from their agonizing physical death any more than Jesus was. But one of them died cursing while the other died on his way to paradise with Christ, because he turned in faith to Jesus. Neither was saved physically, but one was saved eternally. Even he, however, was not saved from the cross he was nailed to.

On the other hand, the opposite possibility exists also. That is, it is possible to benefit from the blessings of God's saving activity in history and yet not respond in repentance, faith and obedience and thereby enter into eternal salvation. God can do amazing things for people—things that the Bible can describe in salvation language—and yet they may choose the way of rebellion and rejection that leads ultimately to destruction.

Such was the fate of the exodus generation, whom Paul explicitly holds up as a warning of this very thing. They experienced God's deliverance, and the Old Testament explicitly describes the exodus in salvation language, as we have seen. But, Paul, explains,

> I do not want you to be ignorant of the fact, brothers, that our forefathers were all under the cloud and that they all passed through the sea. They were all baptized into Moses in the cloud and in the sea. They all ate the same spiritual food and drank the same spiritual drink; for they drank from the spiritual rock that accompanied them, and that rock was Christ. Nevertheless, God was not pleased with most of them; their bodies were scattered over the desert. (1 Cor 10:1-5; see the whole context)

And it appears to have been true of many in the Gospel stories. Not all of those who were fed or healed by Jesus necessarily became grateful and repentant followers who entered the kingdom of God. Some people experienced some of the blessings of God's saving power through Christ, but they did not turn to him for salvation from the deepest need of every human heart.

So then, we need to preserve the wholeness of what the Bible teaches about salvation, and the rich tapestry of all that it includes within the range of that vocabulary. But we need to be careful to observe the distinction that the Bible itself makes between the assurance of salvation in relation to the eternal consequences of sin and the recognition that while God is certainly able to deliver from many "dangers, trials and snares" in this life, he does not always do so. Like Shadrach, Meshach and Abednego, we need to balance two equally strong affirmations:

• Our God is fully *able* to save us (from physical danger and death).

• But even if he *does not* . . .

We affirm the *total ability* of God to save; but we affirm equally the *total freedom* of God to do as he choses. That is his sovereignty in salvation. All salvation, at every level and every dimension, "belongs to our God, who sits on the throne."

Our response to such situations needs to be the same as that of the apostle Paul. Three times he pleaded with God to deliver him from his "thorn in the flesh." But God did not, promising rather to provide the grace necessary to bear it.

> But he said to me, "My grace is sufficient for you, for my power is made perfect in weakness." Therefore I will boast all the more gladly about my weaknesses, so that Christ's power may rest on me. That is why, for Christ's sake, I delight in weaknesses, in insults, in hardships, in persecutions, in difficulties. For when I am weak, then I am strong. (2 Cor 12:9-10)

Questions for Reflection or Discussion

1. How does the sovereignty and universality of God strengthen your motivation and justification for mission?

2. How does the Old Testament vision for the inclusion of the nations into an expanded Israel and Zion affect your understanding of (a) the New Testament theology and practice of mission, and (b) your own view of God's future plan for the nations and the mission of the church?

3. What is your assessment of the two views on the destiny of the unevangelized, including unevangelized ancestors? Make sure your own view is grounded on the clear teaching of the Bible. On this difficult issue, how much can we confidently assert, and what should we leave in the hands of God?

4. What would you say to someone who claimed that healing from illness and rescue from poverty are guaranteed now by the promises of God, as much as eternal salvation? What biblical material would you use in tackling this issue?

7

Salvation and the Lamb of God

WE COME BACK FOR THE LAST TIME TO OUR CONTROL TEXT. The great crowd from all nations gathered around the throne of God cry out, "Salvation belongs to our God, who sits on the throne, *and to the Lamb!*" (Rev 7:10, my italics).

In the chapters so far we have looked at various dimensions of this great text. We have noted how it is theocentric, covenantal and historical. We have thought about how it addresses our human need and how it is received in human experience. We have seen how it connects salvation with the blessing of God and the sovereignty of God. Here finally we come to the *Christocentric* dimension of biblical salvation. The salvation which belongs exclusively to "our God"—the biblical God of the biblical covenants—belongs just as exclusively to the Lamb of God, for he is the one through whom God has accomplished his sovereign saving will.

JESUS—THE SAVING GOD

The earliest followers of Jesus—his own disciples and the first believers after Pentecost—were Jews. They knew that Yahweh alone is God and there is no other source of salvation among the gods or on the earth.

They knew this because their Bible told them so, not least Deuteronomy and Isaiah, as we have seen. Nothing was more foundational to their whole worldview and sense of personal identity and security than this truth: *Yahweh is the saving God and there is no other.*

So we can see how amazing it is that they were able to make the same affirmation about Jesus. They became so utterly convinced that Jesus of Nazareth, their own contemporary, shared the very identity of Yahweh their God that they were able to use the same exclusive language of salvation about him. Jesus can do and does do what their core creed told them only God could do. Jesus saves. Daniel's three friends had told Nebuchadnezzar, "the God we serve is *able to save*" (Dan 3:17, my italics). The writer to the Hebrews told his readers, "he [Jesus] is *able to save* completely those who come to God through him" (Heb 7:25, my italics).

Even in his lifetime, the actions of Jesus raised the question of how he was claiming to do what only God could do—that is, to forgive sins (Mk 2:1-12). And repeatedly he told people that their faith had saved them, in ways which included physical healing, but seemed to go well beyond that—as for example when he declared that salvation had come to the house of Zacchaeus on account of the response he had made to Jesus. His very mission, said Jesus, was "to seek *and to save* what was lost" (Lk 19:10, my italics).

What made Jesus' words and actions all the more scandalous was not only this implied claim to be doing what only God could do but that he bypassed the temple in the process. The temple, with its priesthood and sacrifices, was the standard, approved and indispensable focus for forgiveness in Israel's religious system at that time. But Jesus pronounced forgiveness and salvation totally on his own authority and without recourse to the temple system.

In Acts, in the courts of the temple itself, Peter declared that salvation is now to be found exclusively in Jesus. Jesus has become the new temple—the locus of all salvation.

Salvation is found in no one else, for there is no other name under heaven given to men by which we must be saved. (Acts 4:12)

This is consistent with all the preaching recorded in that book, whether by Peter or Paul.

Peter replied, "Repent and be baptized, every one of you, in the name of Jesus Christ for the forgiveness of your sins. And you will receive the gift of the Holy Spirit. (Acts 2:38)

God exalted him [Jesus] to his own right hand as Prince and Savior that he might give repentance and forgiveness of sins to Israel. (Acts 5:31)

Therefore, my brothers, I want you to know that through Jesus the forgiveness of sins is proclaimed to you. (Acts 13:38)

The saving grace of Jesus (expressed in terms that the Old Testament would have applied only to Yahweh) is among the earliest doctrinal agreements in the church. The very first council of the church, in Jerusalem, recorded this as its settled resolution: "We believe it is through the grace of our Lord Jesus that we [Jews] are saved, just as they [Gentiles] are" (Acts 15:11).

Later, another Jewish believer, writing the letter to the Hebrews, describes Jesus as the author or pioneer of salvation (Heb 2:10), the source of our eternal salvation (Heb 5:9) and the mediator of complete salvation for all who come to God through him (Heb 7:25).

Biblical salvation is utterly Christ-shaped. Jesus embodies in his own person the truth of his own name: "Yahweh is salvation."

JESUS—THE LAMB WHO WAS SLAIN

"Salvation belongs to . . . the Lamb." When the Lamb first makes his appearance in John's great vision, two things are said about him. "Then I saw a Lamb, looking as if it had been slain, standing in the center of the throne" (Rev 5:6).

He is the Lamb who was slain, and simultaneously the Lamb upon the throne. The first image points to Jesus as the crucified Savior. The second image points to Jesus as the risen, ascended and reigning Savior. Both are essential, of course, to the salvation that belongs to our God and to the Lamb. So we need to consider both, focusing first on the cross.

Salvation belongs to the Lamb who was slain because the source and ground of our salvation is the historical, once-for-all atonement achieved by Jesus on the cross. Christianity without the cross would be Christianity without salvation.

The cross is central to God's plan in history. The first action of the Lamb in John's vision is to take the scroll from the hand of God and begin to open its seven seals. The scroll appears to stand for the whole of human history—but not merely as a chronology of one thing after another. Rather, the scroll speaks of the purpose of God within history. History has a meaning and purpose, but what is it? Philosophers and historians have wrestled with that question, but none of them, or any of us, has the leverage to interpret the whole of history and explain the mind of God within it. So who is worthy to do so? The Lamb of God— that is to say, the *crucified* Jesus. Jesus and the cross provide the central key to the whole meaning of human history within the plan of God. Why is this so? Why is the *crucified* Jesus the key to the meaning of history? The song that John immediately hears explains it.

> And they sang a new song:
> "You are worthy to take the scroll
>   and to open its seals,
> because you were slain,
>   and with your blood you purchased men for God
>   from every tribe and language and people and nation.
> You have made them to be a kingdom and priests to serve our God,
>   and they will reign on the earth." (Rev 5:9-10)

The cross is central and key to God's plan for all history for three reasons within this song.

It is redemptive. Through the death of Christ, God has redeemed people ("you purchased men for God"). So humanity will not simply "go down the drain." History has a redemptive ending, because of the cross.

It is universal. Through the death of Christ, God fulfilled his promise to Abraham that he would bless all the nations. Those redeemed by the cross will be drawn from "every tribe and language and people and nation." History is filled with hope and meaning because salvation is available for people of all nations and cultures, everywhere, because of the cross.

It is victorious. Through the death of Christ, God has achieved victory over all that opposes and seeks to destroy his people. They will share in the kingdom of God, that is, through the reign of Christ. The Lamb wins! History belongs to the kingdom of God.

The cross accomplished God's mission for the whole creation. The Bible presents to us God's mission to redeem and renew his whole creation. We have already glimpsed something of the great contours of that in the Old Testament revelation. And every dimension of that mission of God led inexorably to the cross of Christ. The cross was the unavoidable cost of God's mission. It would be impossible in this short space to fathom the depths of what God accomplished through the cross of Christ, and many books have been written seeking to do so. However, let us at least set out some of the most prominent aspects. What does the Bible show us about the grand plan of God for the salvation of humanity and the redemption of creation?

Dealing with the problem of human sin. The effect of sin on each human person is comprehensively described in the Bible, and the extent of what God accomplished on the cross is correspondingly extensive. The Bible uses different metaphors to express the ontological reality of the atonement. It is important not to think of these as mere metaphors—as if they were not referring to something real. The atonement is a great, cosmic *reality*—an achievement that stands as the greatest truth in the universe. But the breadth and depth of that atonement is greater than can be captured in a single way. Among the key concepts are these:[1]

- *Justification.* Sin makes us guilty before God and deserving of God's punishment. At the cross God took that guilt and punishment upon himself in the person of his own Son. For "the LORD has laid on him the iniquity of us all" (Is 53:6), and "[Christ] himself bore our sins in his body on the tree" (1 Pet 2:24). We thus stand before God *not* guilty, in the righteousness of Christ. Through the substitutionary death of Christ, we are put right with God. For "God made him who had no sin to be sin for us, so that in him we might become the righteousness of God" (2 Cor 5:21).

- *Redemption/ransom.* Sin puts us into slavery, a bondage from which we need to be released. But redemption implies a cost. God bore that cost himself in the self-giving of his Son, who came "to give his life as a ransom for many" (Mk 10:45). "In him," therefore, "we have redemption through his blood, the forgiveness of sins" (Eph 1:7).

- *Reconciliation.* Sin makes us enemies of God. There needs to be reconciliation that removes that enmity. That too was part of the accomplishment of the cross. "For if, when we were God's enemies, we were reconciled to him through the death of his Son, how much more, having been reconciled, shall we be saved through his life! Not only is this so, but we also rejoice in God through our Lord Jesus Christ, through whom we have now received reconciliation" (Rom 5:10-11).

- *Cleansing.* Sin makes us dirty. Uncleanness in the Old Testament was a state in which it was impossible to come into the presence of God. Among the effects of the blood of animal sacrifices was to remove uncleanness and enable a person to come back into fellowship with God and the assembly of his people. The New Testament speaks of the cleansing power of the sacrificial blood of Christ—which is one aspect of calling him "the Lamb of God." "The blood of Jesus, his Son, cleanses us from all sin. . . . If we confess our sins, he is faithful and just and will forgive us our sins and cleanse us from all unrighteous-

ness. . . . He is the atoning sacrifice for our sins, and not for ours only
but also for the sins of the whole world" (1 Jn 1:7–2:2 NRSV).

So in these ways, the consequences of sin in our individual lives have
been dealt with by God through the cross of Christ. From being guilty,
enslaved, enemies and unclean, the blood of Christ brings us righteousness, freedom, reconciliation and cleansing.

Defeating the powers of evil. From Genesis 3 onward, the Bible shows
that evil in the world is more than merely a human reality. We are, of
course, entirely responsible before God for the guilt of our own sinful
choices. But human sin is bound up with satanic evil. The Bible teaches
us that there are evil forces, fallen and rebellious angels (remembering
that angels too are part of God's creation—not "gods"), which oppress,
crush, invade and spoil human life. The Bible gives us no clearly revealed
explanation for the *origin* of evil within God's good creation. But it gives
unmistakably clear teaching on the ultimate *destiny* of all evil forces—
and that is their utter and total destruction. This too is the accomplishment of God through the cross of Christ, where, "having disarmed the
powers and authorities, he made a public spectacle of them, triumphing
over them by the cross" (Col 2:15). The victory of the cross will be sealed
by the final destruction of Satan, as portrayed in Revelation. The cross is
the great cosmic victory of God through Christ.

Destroying death. Death is the great invader and enemy of human life
in God's world. Since the garden of Eden, we have been subject to death,
both physically and spiritually. That is, not only are we in any case mortal, we are also spiritually dead in sin, cut off from the life of God (Eph
2:1). So we need a salvation that deals with the reality of death in its full-
est sense. And this too is what God accomplished and offers us through
the cross, "so that by [Christ's] death he might destroy him who holds
the power of death—that is, the devil" (Heb 2:14). The cross thus also
becomes the gateway to new life, that is, into the resurrection life of
Christ, which is the life of God. "God, who is rich in mercy, *made us alive*

with Christ even when we were dead in transgressions—it is by grace you have been saved" (Eph 2:4-5, my italics). Thus, salvation also includes regeneration and new birth.

Removing the barrier of enmity and alienation. Sin introduced enmity into life on earth, starting with the primal enmity between the serpent and the descendants of Adam and Eve. Enmity then becomes a feature of life between human beings as the following narratives show. God's plan of salvation involved the call of Abraham and creation of a new people, Israel, through whom he would bless all nations. But in the Old Testament period God called this people to maintain their holiness—that is, their distinctiveness from other nations. This was the great barrier between Jews and Gentiles, symbolized in the clean and unclean regulations and sustained (on the Jewish side) by strict observance of the law.

God's plan, however, had always been to bless and include all nations among his people (as we saw in chapter six). So eventually the barrier between Jews and Gentiles must also be destroyed. And that is exactly what the cross accomplished. Those who were far off, alienated from the life of God's people and all the promises and hope they shared, are brought near, brought into the very presence of God, through the cross. Three times Paul uses the word *peace* in a short passage in Ephesians that describes this process. Christ *is* our peace; Christ has *made* peace; and Christ came and *preached* peace—and all of this is through the cross.

> But now in Christ Jesus you who once were far away have been brought near through the blood of Christ.
>
> For he himself is our peace, who has made the two one and has destroyed the barrier, the dividing wall of hostility, by abolishing in his flesh the law with its commandments and regulations. His purpose was to create in himself one new man out of the two, thus making peace, and in this one body to reconcile both of them to God through the cross, by which he put to death their hostility. He came and preached peace to you who were far away and peace to those who were near. For through him we both have access to the Father by one Spirit. (Eph 2:13-18)

Thus, a powerful part of the message of the gospel is the reconciliation it enables—reconciliation with God and between human enemies.

Healing and reconciling his whole creation. The Bible teaches that human sin and satanic evil have affected more than just human beings. Creation itself is affected. There is a brokenness and twistedness permeating the creation. We hear of it as early as Genesis 3 when God declares, "Cursed is the ground because of you; through painful toil you will eat of it all the days of your life" (Gen 3:17). And Paul explains it more fully:

> The creation waits in eager expectation for the sons of God to be revealed.
> For the creation was subjected to frustration, not by its own choice, but
> by the will of the one who subjected it, in hope that the creation itself will
> be liberated from its bondage to decay and brought into the glorious free-
> dom of the children of God. (Rom 8:19-21)

God's purpose encompasses his whole creation. God's plan of salvation includes bringing the whole of creation to a new, restored unity in Christ (Eph 1:9-10). This is the cosmic mission of God. And at the cross God accomplished this, in anticipation, even though we do not yet see it finally completed. Paul explicitly links the cross with this cosmic, creational purpose of God in a remarkable passage in which he uses the phrase "all things" five times to describe the whole creation.

> He is the image of the invisible God, the firstborn over all creation. For
> by him *all things* were created: things in heaven and on earth, visible and
> invisible, whether thrones or powers or rulers or authorities; *all things*
> were created by him and for him. He is before *all things,* and in him *all*
> *things* hold together. And he is the head of the body, the church; he is the
> beginning and the firstborn from among the dead, so that in everything
> he might have the supremacy. For God was pleased to have all his fullness
> dwell in him, and through him to reconcile to himself *all things,* whether
> things on earth or things in heaven, by making peace through his blood,
> shed on the cross. (Col 1:15-20, my italics)

So "all things" that have been created by Christ and are being sustained by Christ have been reconciled by Christ, through the cross. This is the incredible creational scope of Paul's understanding of God's salvation.

So then, all these huge dimensions of God's plan of salvation are set before us in the Bible. God's mission was that

- sin should be punished and sinners forgiven
- evil should be defeated and humanity liberated
- death should be destroyed and life and immortality brought to light
- enemies should be reconciled, to one another and to God
- creation itself should be restored and reconciled to its creator

And all of these led to the cross of Christ. The cross was the unavoidable cost of God's mission—as Jesus himself accepted, in his agony in Gethsemane: "Yet not as I will, but as you will" (Mt 26:39). So as we get our minds around the biblical concept of salvation, let us make room for all that the Bible teaches. Salvation, we have reminded ourselves often in this book, is not just a theory, a doctrine, or a merely subjective state or experience. Salvation is what God has done. Biblical salvation is the historic reality that God sent his Son into the world and his Son willingly gave up his life on the cross in fulfillment of that mission. It was the unfathomable determination of the saving love of God that led to those six hours on a Friday outside Jerusalem; to that bleeding body stretched on two pieces of wood; to a torn curtain and a quaking earth; to that awful cry of dereliction, "My God, my God, why have you forsaken me?" (Mt 27:46); and to that triumphant shout of achievement, "It is finished!" (Jn 19:30). For it was indeed on the cross that Jesus accomplished the mission of God, for "*God* was in Christ, reconciling the world unto himself" (2 Cor 5:19 KJV, my italics).

And let us remember, also, that a full biblical understanding of the atonement (of which the above points are the merest sketch) goes far beyond the matter of *personal* guilt and *individual* forgiveness—though

of course it includes them. To know that Jesus died in my place, bearing the guilt of my sin, as my voluntary substitute, is the most glori-
ously liberating truth, to which I cling in glad and grateful worship
with tears of wonder. That I should long for others to know this truth,
and be saved and forgiven by casting their sins on him in repentance
and faith, is the most energizing motive for evangelism. But there is
more in the biblical theology of the cross than individual salvation, and
there is more to mission than evangelism. The gospel is good news for
the whole creation. When we list all those other dimensions of God's
redemptive plan (as we just did above), we are not watering down the
gospel of personal salvation, but rather setting it affirmatively within
its full biblical context of all that God has achieved and will finally
complete, through the cross of Christ.

   The cross shapes the whole of our mission. So, we have seen that the
cross was the unavoidable cost of *God's* mission. But it is equally true,
and biblical, to say that the cross is the unavoidable center of *our* mission. *All Christian mission flows from the cross*—as its source, as its power
and as that which defines its scope.

   It is vital that we see the cross as central to every aspect of holistic, biblical mission—that is, at the center of all we do in the name of the crucified and risen Jesus. It is a mistake, in my view, to think that while our
evangelism must be centered on the cross (as of course it has to be), our
social engagement and other forms of practical mission work have some
other theological foundation or justification. Why is this so? It is because
in all forms of Christian mission in the name of Christ we are confronting
the powers of evil and the kingdom of Satan—with all their dismal effects
on human life and the wider creation. If we are to proclaim and demonstrate the reality of the reign of God in Christ—that God is king, in a
world which likes still to chant "we have no king but Caesar" and his
many successors, including mammon—then we will be in direct conflict
with the usurped reign of the evil one, in all its legion manifestations.

   This is the unanimous testimony of those who struggle for justice, for the needs of the poor and oppressed, the sick and the ignorant, as much as those (frequently the same people) who struggle evangelistically to bring people to faith in Christ as Savior and Lord. In all such work we confront the reality of sin and evil, challenging the darkness of the world with the light and good news of Jesus Christ and the rich totality of salvation that God offers through him.

By what authority can we do so? With what power are we competent to engage the powers of evil? On what basis can we challenge the chains of Satan, in word and deed? Only the cross is sufficient. Only in the cross is there forgiveness of sin, the defeat of evil powers, release from the fear of death, the reconciling of enemies, the healing of creation.

The fact is that sin and evil constitute bad news in every area of life on this planet. The saving work of God through the cross of Christ is good news for every area of life touched by sin—which means every area of life. Bluntly, we need a holistic gospel and a holistic mission because the world is in a holistic mess. And by God's incredible grace we have a gospel big enough for all that sin and evil has touched. And every dimension of that good news is good news utterly and only because of the blood of Christ on the cross. Ultimately all that will be there in the new and redeemed creation will be there because of the cross. And conversely, all that will *not* be there (suffering, tears, sin, corruption, decay and death) will not be there because they will have been destroyed by the cross.

So it is my passionate conviction that holistic mission must have a holistic theology of salvation, centered on a holistic theology of the cross. That includes the conviction that the cross must be as central to our social engagement as it is to our evangelism. There is no other power, no other resource, no other name, through which we can offer the whole gospel to the whole person in the whole world, than Christ crucified and risen.

JESUS—THE LAMB ON THE THRONE

Resurrection and the rule of Christ. Salvation also belongs not only to the Lamb who was slain, but equally to the *Lamb on the throne,* because he ever reigns with the Father. The sovereignty of the Lord of the universe is shared with Christ. This is visualized in the rather remarkable way John's vision of the throne of God not only sees it occupied by the Lord God, the creator (Rev. 4:11), but also by the Lamb who is "standing in the center of the throne" (Rev 5:6). The government that is exercised from the throne is simultaneously God's and Christ's. There is, of course, no difference, in view of our understanding of the oneness of the Trinity.

The most quoted Old Testament psalm in the New Testament is used to make this point about Jesus.

> The LORD says to my Lord:
>   "Sit at my right hand
> until I make your enemies
>   a footstool for your feet." (Ps 110:1)

Paul, among others, builds both parts of this verse (the right hand of God; enemies under the feet) into his theology of the ascended rule of Christ. Here is his summary of the present "location" of Jesus Christ.

> That power is like the working of his mighty strength, which he exerted in Christ when he raised him from the dead and seated him at his right hand in the heavenly realms, far above all rule and authority, power and dominion, and every title that can be given, not only in the present age but also in the one to come. And God placed all things under his feet. (Eph 1:19-22)

Where is Jesus now?

- God has raised him from the dead—so he shares the life of God.

- God has seated him at his right hand—so he shares the government of God.

- God has put all things under his feet—so he shares the victory of God.

The crucified Jesus is now the risen and reigning Lord. This is the great complementary truth to all that we studied in the preceding section

about the cross. The resurrection was God's seal of approval on what
Christ had done in his self-giving death on the cross.

The resurrection and our salvation. The resurrection constitutes another vital part of our assurance of salvation, additional to the points I
mentioned in chapter five. For, as Paul says,

> For if, when we were God's enemies, we were reconciled to him through
> the death of his Son, how much more, having been reconciled, shall we
> be saved through his life! (Rom 5:10)

And the resurrection of Jesus provides us with the model for our
own future resurrection to life. It is important not to say things like
"Jesus died and came back to life"—as if he were merely resuscitated
to a prolonged spell of earthly life before dying in the end. Jesus did
not die and "come back." Jesus died and went forward—forward into
the new resurrection life of the age to come. He is the firstfruits of the
new creation. So his resurrection is the guarantee of ours, and of the
whole new creation life we will enjoy with him, when he "will trans-
form our lowly bodies so that they will be like his glorious body" (Phil
3:21).

And of course it is the risen Christ who has sent his Spirit, as he promised, whose primary work (as we saw in chapter five) is to apply God's
salvation in our hearts, bearing witness to our sonship, bearing fruit in
our lives, strengthening and comforting us in our witness to Christ.

The resurrection and Christ's universal Lordship. In Philippians 2:6-
11, Paul was quite probably quoting from an early Christian hymn about
Jesus, which shows unmistakably that Jesus was being given the same
honor and worship that was appropriate only for God.

Having described how Jesus humbled himself from glory to the cross,
the hymn goes on, "therefore God has highly exalted him and given him
the name that is above every name." This phrase "the name above every
name" could only mean the personal name of the God of the Old Testament—Yahweh, *ho kyrios,* the LORD.

The intention of granting this name and title to Jesus is that

at the name belonging to Jesus [i.e., probably meaning the name of God, the LORD, that has been given to Jesus, not just the name *Jesus* itself], every knee should bow in heaven and on earth and under the earth, and every tongue confess that Jesus Christ is Lord, to the glory of God the Father. (Phil 2:9-11, my translation)

We are so familiar with this text that we may not have noticed where it comes from. Whoever first composed this stanza has taken a text from Isaiah 45:23-24.

> By myself I have sworn,
>> my mouth has uttered in all integrity
>> a word that will not be revoked:
> Before me every knee will bow;
>> by me every tongue will swear.
> They will say of me, "In the LORD alone
>> are righteousness and strength."

Here Yahweh affirms that all the nations will come to recognize that he alone is God, and that all righteousness (salvation) and strength are to be found in him. Yahweh alone is to be acknowledged and worshiped. And without hesitation, this early Christian hymn writer took those words spoken by God about God and applied them to Jesus.

The uniqueness of Yahweh as the only righteous and saving God is now transformed into the uniqueness of Jesus as the only saving Lord to whom every knee will bow. The two have become one, because in Jesus of Nazareth this saving God has walked among us as our Emmanuel—God with us—and as our Jeshua—God the Savior.

QUESTIONS FOR REFLECTION OR DISCUSSION

1. Has your understanding and preaching of the cross tended to be confined to individual sin and salvation? How has this chapter broadened

your biblical understanding of what God accomplished through the cross of Christ? What difference will you allow this to make in your ministry?

2. If you put the cross at the center of holistic mission (including social action and evangelism), what will be the potential results?

3. Make a list of resolutions (commitments to God) of things that will be different in your life and ministry as a result of reading this book and studying the biblical teaching it has surveyed.

Conclusion

Salvation belongs to our God,
who sits on the throne,
and to the Lamb. (Rev 7:10)

As we have worked our way through the implications of this great text, we have explored and rejoiced in these great truths:

- Biblical salvation belongs to God. It is not ours to achieve, to dispense or to manipulate.

- Biblical salvation is the work of the only true and living God of the biblical revelation. He is the God revealed as Yahweh in the Old Testament and who lived among us as Jesus of Nazareth. He is the God whose very identity and nature are constituted by his will and power to save.

- Biblical salvation has been accomplished through the great story of God's mighty acts in history, spanning the whole time line of the Bible and its key covenants, with its center at the cross of Christ and its climax at the return of Christ.

- Biblical salvation comes to us through the invitation of the gospel to enter into that great story by repentance and faith, to know its blessings and assurance now and to anticipate sharing in its climax along with God's people in every age.

- Biblical salvation impacts the whole of life and death in its scope. It affects time and eternity, this age and the age to come. It is above all salvation from the wrath of God so that we may live eternally with him in the new creation. But it includes many other dimensions of the saving blessing of God in this life.

- Biblical salvation is therefore holistic in its scope and in the mission it generates.

- Biblical salvation is guaranteed by the sovereignty of God and is determined by the sovereign grace of God.

- Biblical salvation has been achieved by the Lamb of God, the Lord Jesus Christ who was slain for us on the cross, rose again for us, is seated at the right hand of God and alone is worthy of all honor and praise.

Our response must surely be to join all the rest of creation in praise and worship.

Then I heard every creature in heaven and on earth and under the earth and on the sea, and all that is in them, singing:

> "To him who sits on the throne and to the Lamb
> be praise and honor and glory and power,
>> for ever and ever!"

The four living creatures said, "Amen," and the elders fell down and worshiped. (Rev 5:13-14)

Notes

Chapter 1: Salvation and Human Need

[1] I. Howard Marshall, "Salvation," in *Dictionary of Jesus and the Gospels: A Compendium of Contemporary Biblical Scholarship,* ed. Joel B. Green et al. (Downers Grove, Ill.: InterVarsity Press; Leicester: Inter-Varsity Press, 1992), p. 723.

Chapter 2: Salvation and God's Unique Identity

[1] Gerald O'Collins, "Salvation," in *Anchor Bible Commentary,* ed. David Noel Freedman (New York: Doubleday, 1992), 5:908.

Chapter 3: Salvation and God's Covenant Blessing

[1] The remainder of this chapter is derived (somewhat modified and abbreviated) from Christopher J. H. Wright, *The Mission of God: Unlocking the Bible's Grand Narrative* (Downers Grove, Ill.: IVP Academic; Leicester: Inter-Varsity Press, 2006), chap. 6.

[2] We will examine the disputed meaning of the final verb later.

[3] Gordon J. Wenham, *Genesis 1-15,* Word Biblical Commentary (Dallas: Word, 1987), p. 275 (my italics).

[4] M. Daniel Carroll, "Blessing the Nations: Toward a Biblical Theology of Mission from Genesis," *Bulletin for Biblical Research* 10 (2000): 29.

[5] See N. T. Wright, *The New Testament and the People of God* (London: SPCK, 1992), p. 262. Wright substantiates this understanding of Abraham and Israel as the new Adam (humanity) widely from rabbinic sources and Old Testament texts.

[6] I have provided a detailed survey of "God and the nations in Old Testament vision" in *Mission of God,* chap. 14.

[7] John Calvin, *Genesis* (Edinburgh: Banner of Truth, 1965), pp. 348-49.

Chapter 4: Salvation and God's Covenant Story

[1] I have surveyed this sequence more fully in *Knowing Jesus Through the Old Testament* (Oxford: Monarch Books; Downers Grove, Ill.: InterVarsity Press, 1995), chap. 2. See also, for a more detailed study of the missional significance of the sequence of covenants in the Bible, Christopher J. H. Wright, *The Mission of God: Unlocking the Bible's Grand Narrative* (Downers Grove, Ill.: IVP Academic; Leicester: Inter-Varsity Press, 2006), chap. 10.

[2] The topic of other religions and how we should assess their truth and salvation claims in relation to the Bible is, of course, a major topic that cannot be adequately handled here. Another volume in the Global Christian Library series is devoted to this topic, however: Ida Glaser, *The*

Bible and Other Faiths: Christian Responsibility in a World of Religions (Downers Grove, Ill.: InterVarsity Press; Leicester: Inter-Varsity Press, 2005). And see also my own survey of some issues, including pluralism, in *The Uniqueness of Jesus,* Thinking Clearly (Oxford: Monarch Books, 1997).

[3]There are religious traditions which emphasize the role of faith and devotion to a particular god or enlightened one, rather than one's own merit (such as in Japanese Pure Land Buddhism and in the more devotional mystic traditions, such as the Bhakti tradition in Hinduism and the Sufi tradition in Islam). Such awareness of the need for divine grace and love is doubtless a mark of the grace of God, and Christian theology of religion needs to engage with and give some account of such phenomena. Nevertheless, the main point of the argument above relates to the predominant popular understanding of religion—namely, that whatever concept of salvation I seek (and there is massive variation among the major faiths on that point), it is the path of religious practice and duty that I must follow that will achieve it.

[4]This is the central argument of my book, *Knowing Jesus Through the Old Testament.*

Chapter 5: Salvation and Our Experience

[1]William Temple, *Nature, Man, and God* (London: Macmillan, 1934), p. 401.

[2]Cecil F. Alexander, "There Is a Green Hill Far Away."

[3]We are "children of God," whether male or female, of course. But when Paul uses *sons,* he is thinking of the rights of inheritance that belonged to the firstborn son, or to a slave that was adopted into that status. Thus, in his metaphor, whether male or female, we have been adopted into the status of "son and heir." The point is about our status in Christ, not about our gender.

Chapter 6: Salvation and the Sovereignty of God

[1]By pluralism here, I mean the religious ideology that affirms that all religions are partially valid, culturally relative and equally effective in helping adherents to achieve salvation (however that may be understood). That kind of religious relativism is excluded by texts like Deuteronomy (and many others of course). However, there is a proper kind of social and political pluralism, in which we recognize the freedom of all people to choose how they wish to worship, and the need to protect their legal right to do so. It is possible, on biblical grounds in my view, to be religiously exclusive in one's truth claims about the biblical revelation and salvation in Christ, while being socially and politically pluralist in expressing "love for neighbor" within human society. This sense of distinction and balance is often misunderstood.

[2]I heard John Stott declaim these words many times in an address he often gave on the theme "Jesus Is Lord: A Call to Radical Discipleship." I am not aware of any exact reference in his writings.

[3]I have discussed the topic of the nations much more fully in Christopher J. H. Wright, *The Mission of God* (Downers Grove, Ill.: IVP Academic; Leicester: Inter-Varsity Press, 2006), chap. 14, and the following section is a modified extract from that chapter.

[4]I have discussed this issue more fully in Christopher J. H. Wright, *The Uniqueness of Jesus* (Oxford: Monarch Books, 1997).

[5]It is important, however, to distinguish between motivation that is *effective* (as this belief cer-

tainly is as a motivation for evangelism) and motivation that is actually *true* (i.e., unequivocally based on what the Bible clearly teaches).

[6]It is questionable, however, whether this text can be used to assert that salvation can *only* come through Christian evangelism. In the context, it is clear Paul is talking primarily about what Old Testament Israelites had known and heard, through which they could and should have responded in saving faith.

Chapter 7: Salvation and the Lamb of God

[1]For more extensive study of the atonement, readers will need to consult fuller works of biblical and systematic theology.

Scripture Index

Genesis
1, 63
1–11, 58
1:28, 64
2:24, 65
3, 58, 184, 186
3–11, 58
3:15, 58, 70
3:17, 186
5:2, 64
6–9, 60
8:20–9:17, 88
8:21-22, 88
9, 63
9:1, 64
9:8-17, 88
10, 60, 61, 63
11, 58, 60, 61, 96
12, 58, 60, 61
12:1-3, 58, 59, 62,
  63, 68, 69, 70, 71,
  84, 85, 89
12:3, 61, 78
14:18-20, 68
15, 89
15:6, 164
15:17, 89
17, 126
18:18, 78
18:25, 171
22, 67
22:16-18, 70
22:18, 78
24:1, 64
24:35-36, 64
26:3, 64
26:4-5, 78
26:29, 66
28:14, 78
30:27-30, 68
32:26-29, 67

35:9, 64
39:5, 64, 68
47:7, 68
47:10, 68
48:15-16, 67
48:20, 78
49:24-26, 68

Exodus
1:7, 90
2:23-25, 101
2:24, 90
3:6, 90
3:7-8, 18
3:15, 90
6:2-8, 90
12, 99
15:2, 49
19, 75, 91
19:3-6, 75
19:4-6, 91
20, 91
22:1, 29
24, 91

Leviticus
26:4-13, 64
26:11-12, 64

Deuteronomy
4:32-35, 45
4:33, 45
4:34, 45
4:35, 46, 122, 123
4:39, 45, 46
6:4-5, 57
6:20-25, 100
6:21, 127
8, 77
10:14, 38, 140,
  141, 145

10:14-19, 139
10:15, 140
10:17, 140, 141
10:19, 140
23:1-8, 153
26:1-11, 100,
  131
26:17-18, 57
28:3-15, 64
28:9-10, 155
29:29, 170
30, 75, 103
32:15, 50

Joshua
2, 165

Judges
2:15-16, 19
2:18, 19
6, 52
6:14-15, 41
6:31, 52
7:2, 41
7:7, 41
10:11-14, 41

Ruth
1:16-17, 165
4:11-12, 78

1 Samuel
17:47, 41

2 Samuel
6:2, 155
7, 91
7:8-16, 92

1 Kings
8:43, 155

17:24, 165
21, 48

2 Kings
5:15-18, 165

Psalms
2:10-11, 81
7:1-2, 20
7:10, 20
18:2, 50
20:6-9, 19
22:27-28, 81
27:1, 133
27:13, 133
32:1-2, 26
33:16-17, 42
33:16-19, 19
36:6, 50
42:5, 50
46:1, 101
51:1-3, 26
62:6-7, 50
68:31-32, 81
72:4, 21
72:13, 21
72:17, 78
76:8-9, 21
86:8-10, 81
86:9, 166, 167
87, 81, 156
87:3-6, 147
87:4, 147
89:26, 50
95:1, 50
96:1-3, 81
102:15, 81
102:21-22, 81
103:10-12, 26
110:1, 190
117:1-2, 81

138:4-5, 81
145:10-12, 81
145:18-20, 119
146:3, 42
148:11, 81

Isaiah
2:1-5, 81
6, 138
12:4-5, 81
18:7, 81
19, 150
19:1-17, 149
19:16-25, 81
19:18-22, 149
19:19-25, 149, 151
19:20-22, 151
19:23, 150
19:25, 152
23:17-18, 81
24:14-16, 81
25:7-8, 27
25:9, 119
30:15, 119
38, 19
38:6, 19
38:20, 19
40, 29
40–45, 143
40:22, 142
42:6, 94
42:10-12, 81
43, 49
43:3, 50
43:9-12, 111
43:10, 102
43:11-13, 43
43:25, 26
44:6, 102
44:9-20, 53
44:16-17, 53
44:20, 53
45, 144

45:6, 81
45:14, 81
45:20-21, 43
45:20-24, 143
45:21, 144
45:23-24, 192
46:1-7, 52
46:3-4, 53
46:7, 53
46:10, 102
47:13-14, 42
49:6, 94
53:6, 183
53:10-12, 27
54:7-10, 94
55:3-5, 94
56:3-7, 152
56:3-8, 81
56:4-6, 153
59:15-17, 42
60, 81
61:5-7, 81
63:19, 155
66:18-19, 81

Jeremiah
2:27-28, 54
15:20-21, 20
25:29, 155
31:31-34, 93, 94

Ezekiel
1, 138
5:5-7, 113
14:14, 165
14:20, 165
33:11, 170
34:23-31, 94
36:24-28, 27
37, 27

Daniel
3:17, 174, 179

3:18, 174
9:24, 27

Hosea
13:4, 47

Joel
2:32, 104, 121

Amos
1–2, 154, 155
3:2, 60
5:18-24, 103
9:11-12, 81, 154

Micah
7:18, 28

Zephaniah
3:9, 104
3:14-17, 104

Zechariah
2:3-5, 156
2:8-9, 156
2:10-11, 155
2:10-12, 81
9:7, 81
13:1, 27

Matthew
1:21, 28, 50
3:6, 28
5:14-16, 113
8:24-25, 22
14:30, 22
19:16, 29
19:23, 29
19:25, 29
26:39, 187
27:46, 187
28:18, 141
28:18-19, 145

28:18-20, 70

Mark
2:1-12, 23, 179
3:1-5, 23
10:45, 183

Luke
1:47, 28
1:69, 28
1:71, 28
1:77, 28
2:11, 28
2:30, 29, 51
3:6, 29
7:36-50, 23
8:12, 124
18:14, 167
19:8-10, 29
19:10, 179
22:18, 128
22:20, 95
23:35-39, 23
24:44-47, 114
24:45-48, 112

John
1:29, 28
3:16-17, 30
4:22, 30
4:42, 30
5:31-40, 124
11:11-12, 22
12:47-48, 31
13:35, 113
14:6, 161
16:8-10, 135
17:3, 47
19:30, 187

Acts
1:8, 112
2:14-21, 104

2:38, *180*
3:19-21, *105*
4:4-16, *46*
4:8-12, *46*
4:12, *47, 161, 180*
5:31, *180*
8, *49, 154*
10:44-48, *135*
11:15-18, *120, 135*
13:32-33, *32*
13:38, *180*
14:17, *109*
15:11, *180*
17:26, *60*
17:26-27, *163*
17:27, *109*

Romans
1, *79, 109*
1:18-21, *163*
3:23, *33, 162*
4:3, *164*
4:16-17, *89*
5:9-10, *105*
5:10, *191*
5:10-11, *183*
5:19, *70*
6:1-4, *126*
8, *134*
8:15-17, *136*
8:19-21, *186*
8:23-24, *101*
8:28-30, *135*
8:35-39, *135*
9–11, *106*
9:4-5, *148*
10:1, *32*
10:12-13, *104*
10:13-17, *161*
10:14, *121*
10:17, *122*
11:11, *32*
11:26, *33, 106*

13:11, *105*

1 Corinthians
1:18, *102*
8:5-6, *142*
10:1-2, *126*
10:1-5, *175*
10:1-13, *74*
11:26, *128*
15, *131*
15:1-6, *132*
15:2, *124*

2 Corinthians
1:8-10, *24*
2:15, *102*
5:19, *130, 187*
5:21, *183*
12:9-10, *176*

Galatians
2:20, *123*
3, *70, 83*
3:8, *84, 165*
3:9, *84*
3:26-29, *84*
5:22-26, *136*

Ephesians
1, *61*
1:3, *61*
1:7, *183*
1:9-10, *186*
1:19-22, *190*
2–3, *83*
2:1, *184*
2:1-3, *33*
2:4-5, *185*
2:4-10, *33, 120*
2:8-9, *33, 101*
2:11-12, *33*
2:12-13, *153*
2:13, *34*

2:13-18, *185*
2:14-18, *34*
2:19-22, *34*
3:6, *152*
3:18, *10*

Philippians
2:6-11, *191*
2:9-11, *192*
2:12-13, *102*
3:2-11, *149*
3:20, *105*
3:21, *191*

Colossians
1:13, *101*
1:15-18, *141*
1:15-20, *186*
2:11-12, *126*
2:15, *184*

1 Thessalonians
1:9, *84*

2 Thessalonians
2:13-14, *97, 98*

1 Timothy
1:15, *35*
4:1-5, *66*
5:3-10, *66*

2 Timothy
2:19, *170*
3:15, *124*

Titus
2:9-10, *113*
3:5, *101, 127*

Hebrews
1:2, *141*
2:10, *180*

2:14, *184*
5:9, *180*
6:13-19, *133*
7:25, *179, 180*
11, *133, 173*
11:5-6, *165*
11:32-35, *173*
11:35, *173*
11:35-38, *173*
11:39-40, *174*

1 Peter
1:4-5, *134*
1:8-9, *134*
2:2, *102*
2:24, *183*

2 Peter
1:4, *132*

1 John
1:7–2:2, *184*
4:13-16, *136*

Revelation
4–7, *138*
5:6, *180, 190*
5:9, *61*
5:9-10, *181*
5:13-14, *195*
7, *58, 106, 142, 144, 145*
7:9, *145, 166, 167*
7:9-10, *16*
7:10, *11, 12, 37, 38, 44, 117, 140, 145, 171, 178, 194*
17:14, *141*
21:3, *95*
21:4, *27*
21:24, *61*
22, *58, 96*
22:2, *61*

John Stott Ministries

The vision of John Stott Ministries (JSM) is to see Majority World churches served by conscientious pastors who sincerely believe, diligently study, relevantly apply and faithfully expound the Word of God.

For over thirty years JSM's Langham programs have helped burgeoning non-Western churches to balance *growth* with *depth*. Three key programs help Majority World church leaders disciple their congregations toward greater spiritual maturity.

JSM-Langham Scholarships have enabled more than 120 Majority World church leaders to study theology at the postgraduate level in the West. Upon completion of their degrees, these church leaders have returned home to train the next generation of pastors in their countries.

JSM-Langham Preaching Seminars gather pastors for instruction in biblical preaching and teaching. These seminars provide intensive training for pastors largely unschooled in Bible exposition, bringing greater skill and clarity to their preaching.

JSM-Langham Literature works with seminaries and Bible colleges in over seventy countries to give needed books to tens of thousands of pastors, many of whom before had nearly empty bookshelves.

You can participate in the global church. Find out more by visiting JSM at <www.johnstott.org> or contacting JSM at <info@johnstott.org>.